Bevelyn Blair's **Everyday** Cakes

Bevelyn Blair's

everyday

cakes

The ultimate workday, weekend, and special occasion cake book!

HILL STREET PRESS Athens, Georgia

A HILL STREET PRESS BOOK

Published in the United States of America by
Hill Street Press LLC
191 East Broad Street, Suite 209
Athens, Georgia 30601-2848 USA
706-613-7200
info@hillstreetpress.com
www.hillstreetpress.com

Hill Street Press is committed to preserving the written word. Every effort is made to print books on acid-free paper with a significant amount of post-consumer recycled content.

Text and cover design by Anne Richmond Boston.

Printed in the United States of America.

Originally published in 1984 as *Country Cakes*. Revised Edition.

Library of Congress Cataloging-in-Publication Data

Blair, Bevelyn.
    [Country cakes.]
    Bevelyn Blair's everyday cakes / Bevelyn Blair.
                p.   cm.
            Originally published: Country cakes. Columbus, Ga : Blair of Columbus, 1984.
            Includes index.
                ISBN 1-892514-61-3 (alk. paper)
                    1. Cake. I. Title.

            TX771 .B55 2000
            641.8'653—dc21   99-088834

            ISBN # 1-892514-61-3

        10 9   8   7   6   5   4   3   2   1

    First printing

contents

We celebrate birthdays and other special occasions with favorite cakes. The highlight of a wedding reception or an anniversary party is always the beautiful cake. Traditional holiday cakes are looked forward to with excitement and remembered with nostalgia.

If you have never baked a cake, begin right now and you will find it easy and gratifying. If you are already an experienced baker, you will no doubt find recipes herein that you have long been searching for! Find a cake that will perfectly satisfy your sweet tooth, then prepare yourself for a joyful experience as you bake the cake of your choice.

Within these pages, you will find a treasured collection of tested cake recipes that I have gathered and developed through years of successful baking. Family and heirloom recipes are included and make this an enticing collection! Baking a cake for someone is paying them the highest of compliments and it is my hope that you will use these cake recipes and will share the results with those you love.

Bevelyn Blair

Bevelyn Blair

cakes & frostings

Every day is the best day for baking a cake.

almond cake

1/2 pound butter, softened
2-1/4 cups sugar
3 cups flour
2-1/2 teaspoons baking powder
1/2 teaspoon salt

1 cup milk
1-1/2 teaspoons vanilla extract
1 cup chopped, blanched almonds
6 egg whites, stiffly beaten

Cream butter and sugar until light and fluffy. Add sifted flour, baking powder, and salt to batter alternately with milk and vanilla extract. Fold in chopped almonds and egg whites. Pour mixture into three or four greased and lightly floured 9-inch pans. Bake at 350°F for approximately 30 minutes or until tests done. Spread **Candied Fruit Icing** between layers and on top and sides.

candied fruit icing

2 cups sugar
1 cup water
4 egg whites, stiffly beaten
1 teaspoon vanilla extract

1/2 cup chopped, candied cherries
1/4 cup chopped, candied pineapple

Boil sugar and water over low heat until syrup spins a thread. Pour slowly into egg whites. Beat mixture until smooth and stiff enough to spread. Add vanilla extract, cherries, and pineapple. Spread between layers and on top and sides of **Almond Cake**.

almond crunch cake

Crust:
1-1/2 cups butter
1-1/2 cups sugar
2 eggs

3 cups sifted cake flour
1/2 teaspoon salt

Cream butter and sugar thoroughly. Add eggs one at a time, blending well after each addition. Add sifted flour and salt and mix until dough forms. Divide in half and spread half in bottom of greased springform pan.

Filling:
1 cup grated or very finely chopped almonds
1/2 cup sugar
1 teaspoon grated lemon zest
1 egg, slightly beaten
Whole almonds for garnish

Blend together all ingredients except whole almonds; spread over crust. Press remaining dough over top of filling and press lightly together. (You may want to make a circle of wax paper the size of the springform pan, and press the dough the size of the circle before placing dough over filling.) Garnish with whole almonds.

Bake at 325°F for 45 to 50 minutes, or until golden brown. Cool and remove from pan. Cut in wedges or diamonds.

. . . .

almond legend cake

1/2 cup chopped almonds
1 cup butter
2 cups sugar
4 eggs, separated
2 tablespoons lemon juice
1 teaspoon grated lemon zest
2 teaspoons vanilla extract
3 cups cake flour

1/4 teaspoon baking soda
2 teaspoons baking powder
1/2 teaspoon salt
1 cup milk
1/4 teaspoon cream of tartar
1/2 cup sugar
1 whole almond

Sprinkle chopped almonds into a well-greased bundt pan; set aside.

Cream butter and sugar together until light and fluffy. Add egg yolks one at a time, beating well after each addition. Add lemon juice, zest, and vanilla extract and continue to beat well. Add sifted dry ingredients to batter alternately with milk.

Beat egg whites and cream of tartar and gradually add 1/2 cup sugar, beating until stiff peaks form. Fold mixture into batter. Pour into pan and press the whole almond just below surface of batter. Bake at 300°F for 1 hour and 20 minutes or until tests done. Cool completely and pour **Lemon Glaze** over cake.

lemon glaze

1 cup sifted confectioners sugar
3 tablespoons lemon juice

Mix ingredients together until well blended.

. . . .

almond cream cake

1-1/2 cups cake flour
2 teaspoons baking powder
1/2 teaspoon salt
1 cup whipping cream
2 eggs
1 cup sugar

1 teaspoon vanilla extract
1 (3-ounce) package cream cheese
1 cup sifted confectioners sugar
1/2 teaspoon almond extract
1 cup slivered almonds, toasted

Sift flour, baking powder, and salt together; set aside. Beat whipping cream until soft peaks form; add eggs one at a time, beating well after each addition. Add 1 cup sugar and beat until smooth and dissolved. Stir in vanilla extract and fold in dry ingredients. Pour into a greased and floured 8-inch square pan. Bake at 350°F for 25 to 30 minutes. Cool.

Beat cream cheese until light and fluffy. Add confectioners sugar and beat until smooth. Add almond extract and blend well. Stir in almonds; spread on cooled cake.

. . . .

almond tea cakes

2-1/2 cups sifted flour
3/4 cup sugar
1/4 teaspoon salt
1 teaspoon baking powder
3/4 cup butter
1 egg

2 tablespoons water
1 teaspoon almond extract
36 whole almonds, blanched
1 egg yolk
1 tablespoon water

Preheat oven to 350°F. Sift flour, sugar, salt, and baking powder together. Using pastry blender or 2 knives, cut in butter until mixture resembles coarse cornmeal. Beat egg with 2 tablespoons water and almond extract. Add to flour mixture, mixing with fork until dough leaves side of bowl. On lightly floured surface, knead dough until smooth. Wrap in waxed paper. Chill 1 hour. Form dough into balls 1 inch in diameter. Place 3 inches apart on ungreased cookie sheets. With palm of hand, flatten each cake to a circle 1/2 inch thick; press almond into center of each. Combine egg yolk with 1 tablespoon water. Brush on cakes. Bake at 350°F for 20 to 25 minutes or until golden brown. Remove to wire rack to cool.

apple cake

1-1/2 cups liquid vegetable
  shortening
2 cups sugar
3 eggs, well beaten
3 cups finely chopped apples
1 cup chopped pecans

3 cups cake flour
1 teaspoon salt
1 teaspoon baking soda
1/2 teaspoon cinnamon
1 teaspoon vanilla extract

Combine shortening and sugar, blending well. Add eggs, apples, and nuts. Sift flour, salt, baking soda, and cinnamon together and add to above mixture. Add vanilla extract. Pour batter into a greased and floured bundt or tube pan. May be baked in 2 loaf pans. Bake at 350°F for 1 hour and 15 minutes. Top with **Glaze for Apple Cake** while cake is in the pan and still hot.

glaze for apple cake

- 1/2 cup butter
- 1 cup light brown sugar
- 1/4 cup milk

In saucepan melt butter and sugar; bring to a boil and cook for 2-1/2 minutes. Add milk and mix well. Pour mixture over hot **Apple Cake**. Let stand in pan for 2 hours before removing cake.

. . . .

cinnamon apple cake

- 2 cups sifted cake flour
- 2 cups sugar
- 2 teaspoons cinnamon
- 1 teaspoon baking soda
- 1/4 teaspoon salt
- 2 eggs

- 1 cup vegetable oil
- 1 teaspoon vanilla extract
- 4 cups chopped apples
- 1/2 cup chopped pecans
- Confectioners sugar

Sift flour, sugar, cinnamon, baking soda, and salt together. Beat eggs and oil until light and foamy. Add vanilla extract. Gradually blend in dry ingredients. Stir in apples and pecans. Pour into greased 13 x 9 x 2-inch cake pan. Bake 350° F for 1 hour. Dust with confectioners sugar.

. . . .

apple pineapple cake

1 (8-ounce) can crushed pineapple
1-1/2 cups sugar
1-1/2 cups vegetable oil
3 eggs
2 cups cake flour
2 teaspoons baking soda

2 teaspoons cinnamon
2 teaspoons vanilla extract
1 teaspoon salt
2 cups apples, peeled and shredded
3/4 cup chopped pecans or walnuts

Drain pineapple thoroughly; reserve 2 tablespoons syrup for frosting. Combine all ingredients well and pour into two greased and floured 9-inch layer cake pans. Bake at 350°F for 35 minutes or until tests done. Cool in pan for 5 minutes.

Turn out on to wire rack and cool completely. Frost between layers and top with **Maple-Flavored Frosting.**

maple-flavored frosting

1 (3-ounces) package cream cheese, softened
2 tablespoons butter, softened
1-1/2 cups confectioners sugar
2 tablespoons reserved pineapple syrup
1/4 cup chopped pecans or walnuts
1/4 teaspoon maple flavoring
Pinch of salt

Blend cream cheese, butter, and confectioners sugar until soft and fluffy. Add pineapple syrup, nuts, maple flavoring, and salt, mixing well. Add more sugar if necessary to make frosting easy to spread.

dutch apple cake

1/3 cup butter
1/2 cup firmly packed brown sugar
1 egg
1 cup cake flour
1 teaspoon baking powder
1 teaspoon cinnamon
1/4 cup milk

4 ounces sharp cheddar cheese,
  shredded
3-1/2 cups apples, peeled and sliced
1/2 cup sugar
1/2 cup pecans, chopped
1 carton whipping cream, whipped
  and sweetened

Beat butter and sugar together until light and fluffy. Add egg, beating well. Sift flour, baking powder, and 1/2 teaspoon cinnamon together. Add to butter and sugar alternately with milk, mixing well after each addition. Stir in 1/2 cup cheese. Pour into a greased 10 x 6-inch baking dish. Combine remaining cinnamon, apples, and sugar; spoon over batter and then sprinkle over the pecans. Bake at 350°F for 35 minutes. Sprinkle over remaining cheese and return to oven until cheese slightly melts. Serve warm topped with whipped cream.

. . . .

apple coconut cake

3 cups cake flour
1 teaspoon baking soda
1 teaspoon salt
1 cup vegetable oil
3 eggs

2-1/4 cups sugar
2 teaspoons vanilla extract
2 cups pecans, chopped
3 cups apples, peeled and chopped
1/2 cup coconut

Combine flour, baking soda, and salt; mix well; set aside. Combine oil, eggs, sugar, and vanilla extract; beat with electric mixer at medium speed for 2 minutes. Add flour mixture; mix at low speed just until blended. Fold in pecans, apples, and coconut. (Batter will be stiff.)

Spoon into a greased and floured 10-inch tube pan. Bake at 350°F for 1 hour and 20 minutes. Cool in pan 10 minutes. Remove from pan; immediately drizzle **Glaze** over cake.

glaze

1/2 cup firmly packed light brown sugar
1/4 cup milk
1/2 cup butter

Combine all ingredients in a heavy saucepan; bring to a full boil and cook, stirring constantly, for 2 minutes. Cool to lukewarm.

. . . .

dried apple cake

2 (6-ounce) packages dried apples
1-3/4 cups water
4 to 5 tablespoons sugar
2 cups firmly packed brown sugar
1 cup butter, melted
2 eggs
1 tablespoon baking soda

4 cups cake flour
1 tablespoon nutmeg
1 tablespoon cinnamon
1 tablespoon ground cloves
1 cup milk
1 (15-ounce) box raisins
1 cup chopped pecans

Combine apples and 1-3/4 cups water in saucepan. Cover and cook until water is absorbed. Cool slightly; mash. Add 4 to 5 tablespoons sugar; set aside. Combine brown sugar, butter, and eggs; beat well. Stir in apples. Combine dry ingredients and add to apple mixture alternately with 1 cup milk, beating well after each addition. Stir in raisins and pecans. Pour batter into a greased 13 x 9 x 2-inch pan. Bake at 350°F for 1 hour.

. . . .

applesauce nut cake

2 cups sifted flour
1 teaspoon baking soda
1 teaspoon baking powder
1 teaspoon cinnamon
1 teaspoon nutmeg
1 teaspoon ground cloves
1/2 teaspoon salt

1/2 cup butter
1 cup sugar
1 egg
1 cup sweetened applesauce
1 teaspoon vanilla extract
3/4 cup raisins
1 cup chopped walnuts or pecans

Sift flour, baking soda, baking powder, cinnamon, nutmeg, cloves, and salt together. Cream butter and sugar together until light and fluffy. Add egg, applesauce, and vanilla extract, blending well. Gradually blend dry ingredients into batter. Stir in raisins and nuts. Pour batter into greased 9 x 5 x 3-inch loaf pan. Bake at 350°F for 55 minutes or until tests done. Cool for 10 minutes.

apple cheese squares

1/2 cup butter
1/3 cup firmly packed brown sugar
1 cup cake flour
1/2 cup finely chopped pecans

2/3 cup apple butter
1 (8-ounce) package cream cheese
1 (7-ounce) jar marshmallow cream
1 egg

Cream butter and sugar until light and fluffy. Add flour and pecans, mixing well. Reserve 1 cup of mixture. Press remaining mixture into bottom of a 9-inch square pan. Bake at 350°F for 15 minutes.

Spread 1/3 of the apple butter over baked crust. (Substitute 2/3 cup applesauce mixed with 1/4 teaspoon cinnamon for apple butter, if necessary.) Combine cream cheese, marshmallow cream, and egg, mixing with electric mixer until well blended. Pour over apple butter and crust.

Top with remaining apple butter and crumb mixture. Bake at 350°F for 45 minutes.

apple pecan cake

1-1/2 cups vegetable oil
2 cups sugar
3 eggs
3 cups cake flour
1 teaspoon salt

1 teaspoon baking soda
3 cups tart apples, diced
1 cup chopped pecans
2 teaspoons vanilla extract

Beat together oil and sugar until light and fluffy. Add eggs one at a time, beating well after each addition. Sift flour, salt, and soda together and add to mixture, blending well. Stir in apples and pecans. Stir in vanilla extract. Pour into a greased tube pan. Bake at 300°F for 1 hour and 15 minutes. While cake is hot, pour **Glaze** over cake.

glaze

1/2 cup butter
1/3 cup milk
1 cup firmly packed light brown sugar

Combine all ingredients and boil for 3 to 4 minutes. Pour over hot cake.

icing for apple cakes

This icing may be used instead of cooked icings, if preferred.

1 (6-ounce) package cream cheese
3 tablespoons butter
1 teaspoon vanilla extract

1-1/2 cups confectioners sugar
Pinch of salt

Using an electric mixer, beat softened cream cheese and butter until smooth. Add remaining ingredients. Spread over cooled cake.

· · · · · · · ·

delicious applesauce cake

1/2 cup butter
1 cup sugar
1 egg, well beaten
1-1/2 cups sweetened applesauce
2 cups flour
2 teaspoons cocoa
1 teaspoon cinnamon

1/2 teaspoon ground cloves
1/8 teaspoon salt
3/4 cup raisins
3/4 cup chopped pecans
2 teaspoons soda
1/4 cup hot water
1 teaspoon vanilla extract

Cream butter and add sugar gradually, creaming until light and fluffy. Add egg and applesauce. Mix well. Sift flour. Measure and sift again with cocoa, cinnamon, cloves, and salt. Mix with raisins and nuts. Add gradually to apple mixture and beat well. Combine soda and hot water; add to mixture and mix well. Add vanilla extract. Bake in two greased and floured layer cake pans at 350°F for 35 minutes. Frost cooled cake with **Caramel-Nut Frosting**.

caramel nut frosting

1-1/2 cups firmly packed light
    brown sugar
1/2 cup granulated sugar
1/4 teaspoon salt

3/4 cup whipping cream
2 tablespoons butter
1 tablespoon cream
1/2 cup chopped nuts

Combine sugars, salt, cream, and butter and bring to a boil, stirring constantly until sugar is dissolved. Cook slowly, keeping crystals scraped from sides of pan. When small amount forms a soft ball (234°F to 240°F) in cold water, remove spoon and set pan aside to cool. Do not move pan until mixture is lukewarm. Beat until thickens. Add cream. Beat until spreading consistency. Add nuts.

covered apple cake

2-1/2 sticks butter
1 cup sugar
5 eggs
1 teaspoon vanilla extract

2 cups cake flour
2 teaspoons baking powder
3 pounds tart apples, peeled and
  sliced

Cream butter and sugar. Add eggs one at a time, mixing well after each addition. Add vanilla extract. Add sifted flour and baking soda one tablespoon at a time. Cream well. Grease and flour a 10-inch springform pan. Put 1/2 the batter in pan and add apples, spreading evenly. Place remaining batter on top. Bake at 350°F for 1 hour and 30 minutes.

While cake is warm, mix 1/2 cup apricot jam and 2 tablespoons water, heat to boiling point and spread over cake. Let cool and mix 1/2 cup confectioners sugar with enough lemon juice to make mixture just thin enough to drizzle over cake.

apple snack cake

3/4 cup vegetable oil
2 eggs
2 cups sugar
2-1/2 cups cake flour
1 teaspoon baking soda
1 teaspoon baking powder

1 teaspoon salt
1 teaspoon cinnamon
3 cups peeled, chopped apples
1 cup chopped pecans
1 (6-ounce) package butterscotch
  morsels

Combine oil, eggs, and sugar in large mixing bowl; beat with electric mixer at medium speed until well mixed. Combine flour, baking soda, baking powder, salt, and cinnamon. Add dry ingredients to batter alternately with apples, mixing well after each addition. Stir in pecans and half the butterscotch morsels. Spread batter into a greased 13 x 9 x 2-inch baking pan. Sprinkle batter with remaining butterscotch morsels. Bake at 350°F for 55 minutes to 1 hour or until tests done.

apple preserve cake

2 cups sifted cake flour
1 teaspoon baking soda
1 teaspoon baking powder
1/4 teaspoon salt
1 teaspoon cinnamon
1 teaspoon nutmeg
1 teaspoon allspice

3/4 cup butter
1 cup sugar
1/2 cup sour cream
1/2 cup apple preserves
3 eggs
1/2 cup chopped pecans

Sift flour, baking soda, baking powder, salt, and spices together 3 times. Cream butter with sugar until fluffy. Add sour cream and apple preserves, mixing well. Add eggs one at a time, beating well after each addition. Add sifted dry ingredients gradually, beating well. Fold in nuts and pour into a greased loaf pan or two greased 9-inch layer cake pans. Bake at 350°F for 50 minutes for loafs or 25 to 30 minutes for layers.

apple upside-down cake

1/4 cup butter
1 cup light brown sugar
2 large baking apples
1-1/2 cups sifted cake flour
1/2 teaspoon salt
3 teaspoons baking powder

1/3 cup butter
1/2 cup granulated sugar
2 eggs, well beaten
1/2 teaspoon vanilla extract
2/3 cup water

Melt 1/4 cup butter in skillet or baking pan. Add brown sugar and stir until melted. Cool. Peel, core, and slice apples and place in bottom of skillet or baking pan. Sift flour, salt, and baking powder together. Cream butter with sugar until fluffy. Add eggs and vanilla extract and beat thoroughly. Add sifted dry ingredients and water to batter alternately in small amounts, beating well after each addition. Pour over apples. Bake at 350°F for 40 to 50 minutes. Turn out on to plate immediately and serve with whipped cream.

apricot nectar cake

4 whole eggs
1 box lemon cake mix
1/2 cup sugar
3/4 cup vegetable oil
1 cup apricot nectar

Juice of 2 lemons
1-1/2 cups confectioners sugar

Beat eggs with electric mixer on high speed; mix with rest of ingredients. Bake in tube pan at 350°F for approximately 1 hour. Cool in pan on wire rack. While cooling, poke holes in cake and pour the juice mixed with confectioners sugar over warm cake .

apricot tea cake

1 cup dried apricots
1 large orange
2 cups flour
1 teaspoon baking soda
2 teaspoons baking powder

1 cup sugar
1/2 cup chopped nuts
1 egg
2 tablespoons butter, melted
1 teaspoon vanilla extract

Simmer apricots in boiling water for 30 minutes. Drain and mash. Squeeze juice from orange. Add enough boiling water to juice to make 1 cup. Sift flour, baking soda, baking powder, and sugar together. Add nuts, fruits, juice, egg, butter, and vanilla extract and mix well. Bake in a greased loaf pan at 350°F for 50 minutes. Serve hot with butter or cold.

arabian ribbon cake

3 cups sifted cake flour
3 teaspoons baking powder

1/4 teaspoon salt
2/3 cup butter

1-1/2 cups sugar
3 egg yolks, well beaten
1 cup milk
3 egg whites, stiffly beaten
1-1/2 teaspoons cinnamon

1/4 teaspoon ground cloves
1/2 teaspoon nutmeg
1/4 teaspoon mace
3 tablespoons dark molasses
Grated lemon zest

Sift flour and measure. Combine baking powder and salt and sift together 3 times. Cream butter thoroughly. Add sugar gradually and cream with butter until light and fluffy. Add egg yolks and beat well. Add flour to batter alternately with milk, a small amount at a time, beating well after each addition. Fold in stiffly beaten egg whites.

Fill one greased 9-inch layer cake pan with 1/3 of the batter. To remaining batter add spices and molasses and blend. Pour into two greased 9-inch layer cake pans. Bake layers at 350°F for 20 to 25 minutes. Place white layer between spice layers. Spread **Fruit Filling** between layers and **Lemon Frosting** on top and sides of cake. Sprinkle grated lemon zest over top of cake.

fruit filling

1 cup water
2 tablespoons butter
Pinch of salt
1 cup finely chopped raisins

1 cup finely chopped figs
1/2 cup finely chopped dates
1 tablespoon lemon juice
1/2 teasoon grated lemon zest

Combine all ingredients in saucepan. Boil slowly 6 to 8 minutes or until thick enough to spread. Cool. Add lemon juice and zest.

lemon frosting

Cream 1 teaspoon grated lemon zest and 4 tablespoons butter together. Gradually add 3 cups confectioners sugar to butter alternately with 3 tablespoons lemon juice, beating well after each addition. Add pinch of salt. If frosting is too stiff to spread, add a little more lemon juice.

apricot cake

1 cup dried apricots
6 tablespoons sugar
2 cups water
1/2 cup butter
1 cup sugar
2 egg yolks

1 teaspoon vanilla extract
1-3/4 cups sifted cake flour
1/2 teaspoon baking soda
1/2 teaspoon salt
1/2 teaspoon baking powder
1/4 cup milk

Simmer apricots, sugar, and water together 30 minutes. Mash and measure 1/2 cup apricot pulp. Cream butter and sugar until light and fluffy. Add yolks and vanilla extract; beat thoroughly. Sift flour, baking soda, salt, and baking powder together 3 times. Add dry ingredients to batter alternately with milk and pulp in small amounts. Bake in greased 8 x 8-inch cake pan at 350°F for 45 minutes or until tests done.

. . . .

apricot chocolate cake

The apricots are just the right touch to set off the chocolate flavor.

Sift together	1-3/4 cups sifted cake flour
	1/2 teaspoon baking powder
	1 teaspoon baking soda
	1 teaspoon salt
	1-1/4 cups sugar
Add	1/2 cup butter
	2/3 cup milk
Beat	for 2 minutes until batter is well blended.
Add	1/3 cup milk; 9 ounces chocolate, melted and cooled; 2 eggs, unbeaten; 1 teaspoon vanilla extract
Beat	for 2 minutes
Fold in	3/4 cup chopped, drained cooked apricots
Pour	into two well-greased and lightly floured pans
Bake	at 350°F for 30 to 35 minutes
Cool	and frost with **Browned Butter Frosting**
Decorate	with pecans

browned butter frosting

1/4 cup butter
1/4 teaspoon salt
4 cups (1 lb.) confectioners sugar
1/3 to 1/2 cup hot cream
1 teaspoon vanilla extract

Brown butter in saucepan; add salt. Blend in confectioners sugar alternately with hot cream. Add vanilla extract. Beat until creamy.

. . . .

banana nut cake

1/2 cup butter
1-1/2 cups sugar
3 egg yolks
1 cup mashed bananas
1/4 cup boiling water
1/2 cup chopped pecans
1 teaspoon lemon juice
2 cups flour
1 teaspoon baking powder
1 teaspoon baking soda, dissolved in 1/4 cup buttermilk
3 egg whites
1/4 teaspoon salt

Cream butter and sugar; add egg yolk and mashed bananas. In separate bowl, pour water over pecans; set aside. Add lemon juice to banana mixture. Sift flour and baking powder together and add to batter alternately with buttermilk and soda mixture. Add pecans. Beat egg whites with salt until stiff peaks form. Fold in egg whites. Bake in two 9-inch layer cake pans at 300°F for 30 to 35 minutes. Spread with **Banana Filling**.

banana filling

1/2 cup butter, softened
1 (16-ounce) box confectioners sugar
1/2 cup mashed bananas
1/2 cup chopped pecans
1 tablespoon orange or lemon juice

Mix butter and sugar until creamy. Add bananas, nuts, and juices. Spread between layers and on sides and top of cake.

. . . .

banana chiffon cake

This cake is moist and delicious. Frost with your favorite Buttercream Icing.

2 cups sifted cake flour
1 cup sugar
1 teaspoon baking powder
1 teaspoon baking soda
1 teaspoon salt
1/3 cup vegetable oil

1 cup mashed bananas
2/3 cup buttermilk
1 teaspoon vanilla extract
2 eggs separated
1/3 cup sugar
1/2 cup chopped pecans

Sift together flour, 1 cup sugar, baking powder, baking soda, and salt. Make a well in center. Pour in oil, bananas, 1/3 cup buttermilk, and vanilla extract. Beat 1 minute, mixing well. Add egg yolks and remaining 1/3 cup buttermilk. Beat 1 minute. Beat egg whites until frothy, gradually beat in 1/3 cup sugar and beat until stiff peaks form; fold into batter. Fold in pecans. Pour into ungreased 9-inch tube pan. Bake at 325°F for 55 minutes.

. . . .

banana split cake

1 cup butter, divided
1-1/2 cups graham cracker crumbs
2 cups confectioners sugar
2 eggs
1 teaspoon vanilla extract
3 or 4 bananas, sliced

1 (20-ounce) can crushed pineapple, drained
1 pint whipping cream, whipped and sweetened to taste
1/2 cup chopped pecans

Melt 1/2 cup butter and add to crumbs. Mix well and pat into a 13 x 9-1/2 x 2-inch pan. Combine sugar, eggs, 1/2 cup softened butter and vanilla extract. Beat until smooth and creamy. Spread over graham cracker crust. Add a layer of banana slices and pineapple; spread whipping cream mixture evenly over fruit. Sprinkle with chopped pecans. Refrigerate until set.

. . . .

berry teacakes

Serve these teacakes while warm and you will find they are a dainty addition to the tea table; try them with butter!

1/4 cup butter, softened
1 cup sugar
2 large eggs
4-1/2 cups cake flour
2 teaspoons baking powder

1/4 teaspoon salt
1-1/2 cups milk
1 pint fresh or 1 (20-ounce can) berries (whole blueberries, cut-up strawberries, etc.)

In a large mixing bowl, cream butter until smooth. Gradually add sugar and beat until blended well. Add eggs, one at a time, beating well after each addition. Sift together 4 cups flour, baking powder, and salt. Add flour mixture alternately with the milk to the butter mixture, beginning and ending with the flour mixture. (If necessary, add additional sifted cake flour to make a stiff batter.) Dredge berries in 1/2 cup flour, then gently stir into batter. Spoon batter into greased muffin tins. Bake at 375°F for approximately 30 to 35 minutes or until golden brown. Recipe yields 24 teacakes. These teacakes freeze well.

. . . .

blueberry mountain cake

2 cups flour
3 teaspoons baking powder
1/4 teaspoon salt
1 cup sugar
1/2 cup shortening

2 eggs, beaten
1 cup milk
1-1/2 cups blueberries
1 cup grated coconut

Sift flour, baking powder, salt, and sugar together; cut in shortening until mixture appears like cornmeal. Combine eggs and milk and mix until just moistened. Fold in blueberries and pour into two 9-inch round greased layer cake pans. Sprinkle coconut on top. Bake at 350°F for approximately 25 minutes.

brownies

1 cup sugar
4 tablespoons cocoa
Pinch of salt
1 cup self-rising flour

1 cup chopped nuts
1 teaspoon vanilla extract
2 eggs
1/2 cup vegetable oil

Mix sugar, cocoa, salt, and flour; add other ingredients, mixing well. Bake at 350°F for 20 minutes. Ice with chocolate icing, if desired, or serve plain. Cut into squares.

burnt sugar cake

1/2 cup sugar
1/2 cup water
1 cup milk
1 cup butter
2 cups sugar
3 eggs

3-1/2 cups plus 1 tablespoon cake
   flour
3 teaspoons baking powder
1 teaspoon salt
1 teaspoon vanilla extract

Put 1/2 cup sugar into hot skillet. Stir constantly until sugar turns to a light brown syrup. Remove from heat. Add water. Return skillet to heat and simmer until just dissolved. Pour syrup—should be 1/2 cup—into measuring cup. Cool, then add milk to make 1-1/2 cups.

Cream butter and sugar until light and fluffy. Add eggs one at a time, beating well after each addition. Stir in vanilla extract. Add sifted dry ingredients to batter alternately with milk and sugar syrup. Pour into greased and floured 9-inch layer cake pans. Bake at 350°F for 24 to 26 minutes. Spread with **Penuche Frosting**.

penuche frosting

2 cups firmly packed light brown sugar
2 cups granulated sugar
2 cups whipping cream
2 tablespoons white Karo syrup
1/2 cup butter, softened

Measure sugars, cream, and syrup into 3-quart saucepan; boil over medium heat, stirring frequently, until sugar dissolves. When syrup reaches steady brisk boil, add butter and cook 20 to 25 minutes or until a small dollop forms soft ball (234°F to 240°F) when dropped in cold water. Cool without stirring. Beat until spreading consistency. If necessary, add cream to thin.

. . . .

black forest cake

2 (15- or 16-ounce) cans pitted tart
  cherries, drained and each fruit
  cut in half
1/2 cup kirsch or other cherry-
  flavor brandy
1 box chocolate cake mix for 2 layer
  cake (or bake a chocolate cake
  from scratch in 3 layers)

9 ounces semi-sweet chocolate
14 maraschino cherries, well drained
2 cups heavy or whipping cream
1/2 cup confectioners sugar

In medium bowl combine tart cherries and 1/3 cup kirsch; set aside, stirring occa-sionally. Prepare cake mix as label directs but pour into three 9-inch round layer cake pans; or bake your own chocolate cake from scratch. Cool on wire racks for 10 minutes; remove from pans; cool completely.

With vegetable peeler, shave a few curls of chocolate for garnish; set aside. Grate remaining chocolate. With fork, prick top of each cake layer. Drain cherries well and slowly spoon the liquid from cherries over cake layers.

Beat cream, sugar, and remaining kirsch until stiff. Place one cake layer on cake plate; spread with 1/4 quantity of whipped cream and top with 1/2 quantity of cherries; repeat with second layer. Top with third layer.

Frost side of cake with remaining whipped cream. Gently press grated chocolate into cream. Garnish top of cake with dollops of remaining cream; top each dollop with a maraschino cherry. Pile chocolate curls in center of cake. Keep refrigerated until ready to serve.

· · · · · · · ·

brown sugar nut cake

1 cup butter	3 cups flour
1/2 cup margarine	2 teaspoons baking powder
1 pound light brown sugar	1 cup milk
1 cup sugar	1 teaspoon vanilla extract
5 eggs	1-1/2 cups chopped pecans

Cream butter, margarine, and sugars until light and fluffy. Add eggs one at a time, beating well after each addition. Add sifted flour and baking powder to batter alternately with milk and vanilla extract. Fold in chopped pecans. Bake in a greased tube pan at 325°F for 1 hour and 30 minutes. Ice with a white icing or serve plain, as desired.

· · · · · · · ·

brown sugar sour cream cake

1 cup butter, softened
2 cups firmly packed light brown
    sugar
2 cups cake flour, measured first,
    then sifted
1 large egg, lightly beaten

1 teaspoon ground nutmeg
1 (8-ounce) carton sour cream,
    combined with 1 teaspoon
    baking soda
1-1/2 cup finely chopped pecans

Combine butter, sugar, and flour. Mix with a wire pastry blender until mixture resembles fine crumbs. In a greased 8-inch springform pan, place half the mixture, pressing firmly over bottom of pan. Combine egg, nutmeg, and sour cream and baking soda mixture, stirring to blend. Add flour mixture to remaining crumb mixture, stirring to combine. Spoon over top of crumb mixture in pan. Sprinkle with chopped pecans. Bake at 325°F for 1 hour or until cake shrinks slightly from edges of pan. Cool completely before removing side of springform pan.

brownie baked alaska

1 quart vanilla ice cream, softened
1/2 cup butter
2 cups sugar, divided
2 eggs
1 cup flour

1/2 teaspoon baking powder
2 tablespoons cocoa
1/4 teaspoon salt
1 teaspoon vanilla extract
5 egg whites

Line a 1-quart mixing bowl with waxed paper, leaving an overhang around edges. Pack ice cream into bowl and freeze until very firm.

Combine butter and 1 cup sugar, creaming until light and fluffy. Add eggs one at a time, beating well after each addition. Sift flour, baking powder, cocoa, and salt; add to creamed mixture, mixing well. Stir in vanilla extract.

Spoon batter into a greased and floured 9-inch round layer cake pan. Bake at 350°F for 25 to 30 minutes. Let cool completely.

Place cake on an ovenproof serving dish. Invert bowl of ice cream onto cake leaving waxed paper intact; remove bowl. Place cake in freezer.

Beat egg whites and gradually beat in 1 cup sugar until stiff peaks form. Remove cake from freezer and peel off waxed paper. Spread meringue over entire surface, making sure edges are sealed.

Bake at 500°F for 2 to 3 minutes or until meringue peaks are browned. Serve immediately.

. . . .

butternut loaves

3-1/2 cups flour	1/2 cup honey
2 teaspoons baking soda	1 cup milk
1 cup chopped pecans	1 teaspoon mace
1 cup vegetable oil	1-1/2 teaspoons nutmeg
2 cups sugar	1-1/2 teaspoons cinnamon
4 eggs	1-1/2 teaspoons salt
1-1/2 cups cooked, mashed butter- nut squash	

Combine flour, baking soda, and pecans and stir well; set aside. Combine oil, sugar, and eggs; beat well. Stir in squash, honey, milk, spices, and salt. Add flour mixture; stir just until all ingredients are moistened.

Pour batter into three greased 9 x 5 x 3-inch loaf pans, or three greased 1-pound coffee cans. Bake at 350°F for 1 hour or until tests done. Cool.

. . . .

brown velvet cake

2 cups sifted cake flour	2 eggs
1 teaspoon baking soda	9 ounces unsweetened chocolate, melted
3/4 teaspoon salt	1 teaspoon vanilla extract
1/2 cup shortening	1 cup, plus 2 tablespoons milk
1-1/2 cups firmly packed brown sugar	

Sift together flour, baking soda, and salt. With an electric mixer, cream together shortening and sugar. Beat in eggs one at a time, beating until mixture is light and fluffy. Stir in chocolate and vanilla extract. Add milk to batter alternately with dry ingredients, beginning and ending with flour. Pour into two greased and floured 9-inch layer cake pans. Bake at 350°F for 25 minutes or until tests done. Cool in pan for 10 minutes; remove to wire rack and finish cooling. Spread cake with your favorite white icing.

. . . .

blueberry buckle

1/4 cup butter, softened
3/4 cup sugar
1 egg
2 cups flour

2 teaspoons baking powder
1/2 teaspoon salt
1/2 cup milk
2 cups blueberries

Cream butter and sugar until light and fluffy. Add egg and beat well. Add sifted dry ingredients to batter alternately with milk, beating until smooth. Fold in berries. Pour into greased 9 x 12-inch pan. Sprinkle with **Crumb Topping**. Bake at 375°F for 35 minutes.

crumb topping

1/4 cup butter
1/2 cup sugar
1/3 cup flour
1/2 tablespoon cinnamon

Cream butter and sugar; add flour and cinnamon. Sprinkle on **Blueberry Buckle** before baking.

. . . .

luscious blueberry cake

3 cups sifted cake flour
2 teaspoons baking powder
1/2 teaspoon salt
1 cup butter
1-1/2 cup sugar
4 eggs, separated
2 teaspoons vanilla extract

2/3 cup milk
1/2 cups sugar
3 cups blueberries (fresh, frozen, or
   canned and drained)
1 tablespoon flour
Confectioners sugar

Sift together flour, baking powder, and salt. Cream butter and 1-1/2 cups sugar until light and fluffy. Add egg yolks and vanilla extract. Blend well. Add dry ingredients to batter alternately with milk. Beat egg whites until stiff peaks form; gradually beat in 1/2 cup sugar. Fold into batter. Combine blueberries and 1 tablespoon flour. Fold into batter. Pour into greased 13 x 9 x 2-inch cake pan. Bake at 350°F for 50 minutes or until tests done. Dust with confectioners sugar.

· · · · · · · · · ·

betsy ross cake

1 cup butter, softened
3 cups sugar
5 eggs, separated
Grated zest and juice of 1 lemon
1/2 teaspoon baking soda
4 cups sifted cake flour

1 cup milk
(To decorate the cake to resemble
   the first American flag, you will
   also need 1 cup hulled blueberries
   and 4 cups hulled strawberries)

Cream butter, adding sugar gradually until light and fluffy. Add egg yolks, zest, juice, baking soda, flour, and milk. Mix until well blended. Beat egg whites stiff but not dry. Fold into batter. Pour into greased and floured 13 x 9 x 4-inch baking pan. Bake at 325°F for approximately 45 minutes or until tests done. Cool cake and spread **White Chocolate Cream Cheese Frosting** over it. Reserve 1/4 of the frosting if decorating as the flag.

white chocolate cream cheese frosting

4 cups confectioners sugar
8 ounces cream cheese
6 ounces white chocolate
2 tablespoons butter
1 teaspoon vanilla extract

Gradually beat sugar into cream cheese until evenly blended. Melt chocolate. Off heat, stir in butter and cool. Blend with cream cheese mixture. Add vanilla extract.

To decorate the cake to resemble the first American flag, arrange drained blueberries in a 4 x 6-inch rectangle in upper left corner of cake. With point of a knife, trace wavy 2-inch stripes from left to right lengthwise across cake. Set strawberries, pointed end up, in alternate stripes. Pipe 13 stars onto blueberries. Pipe remaining frosting onto white stripes

. . . .

butter cake

1 cup chopped pecans
4 eggs
2 cups sugar
1 teaspoon vanilla extract
2 cups flour

1 teaspoon baking powder
1/4 teaspoon salt
1 cup milk
1/2 cup butter

Preheat oven to 350°F. Grease a 9-inch tube pan generously. Line bottom of pan with waxed paper; grease paper. Sprinkle nuts over bottom of pan. Beat eggs until lemon-colored and very thick. Gradually beat in sugar and continue beating until mixture is very thick. Beat in vanilla extract. Mix flour, baking powder, and salt together and blend into batter with electric mixer on lowest speed. Heat milk and butter together in a pan until butter is melted and mixture is boiling. Pour all at once into batter and mix just enough to blend all ingredients together. Immediately pour into prepared pan. Bake at 350°F for approximately 50 minutes. Cool in pan 10 minutes before turning upside down onto a cake plate. Cake will shrink during cooling.

· · · · · · · ·

buttermilk cake

1-3/4 cups butter (3-1/4 sticks)
3-1/3 cups sugar
8 eggs
4-1/2 cups cake flour

1/4 teaspoon baking soda
1 tablespoon vanilla extract
1/2 cup buttermilk

Cream butter and sugar together until very light and fluffy. Add eggs one at a time, beating well after each addition. Add sifted dry ingredients to batter alternately with vanilla extract and buttermilk. Bake in a buttered and lightly floured 10 x 5 x 3-inch loaf pan at 325°F for approximately 1 hour and 15 minutes. Remove to wire rack and immediately turn out onto wire rack carefully to cool, right side up.

· · · · · · · ·

blackberry cake

1/4 cup butter, melted
1 cup sugar
1 egg
2 cups cake flour
1 teaspoon baking powder
1/2 teaspoon baking soda

1/2 teaspoon nutmeg
Pinch of salt
1 cup milk
2 (10-ounce) jars blackberry jam
Confectioners sugar

Cream butter and sugar together until light and fluffy. Add egg, beating well. Beat in sifted dry ingredients alternately with milk. Pour into three greased and floured 9-inch round layer cake pans. Bake at 350°F for 25 to 30 minutes or until tests done. After cakes have been removed from pans and cooled completely, spread blackberry jam between each layer before stacking layers one atop the other. Sift confectioners sugar over the top layer.

black walnut cake

2 cups sifted flour
2-3/4 teaspoons baking powder
1-1/4 teaspoon salt
2/3 cup butter
1-1/2 cups sugar

1 teaspoon vanilla extract
3 eggs, separated
3/4 cup milk
1-1/2 cups black walnuts, chopped
   in small pieces

Sift flour, baking powder, and salt together. Cream butter, sugar, and vanilla extract until fluffy. Add beaten egg yolks. Beat thoroughly. Add sifted dry ingredients to batter alternately with milk in small amounts, beating well after each addition. Add nuts, then the stiffly beaten egg whites. Pour into two greased 9-inch layer cake pans. Bake at 350°F for 30 minutes. When cool, frost with **Caramel Frosting**.

caramel frosting

3 cups sugar
1 cup butter

1 cup milk
1 teaspoon vanilla extract

Combine 1 cup sugar and butter in heavy saucepan or skillet and brown while stirring constantly. In another saucepan, bring 2 cups sugar and milk to a boil and mix slowly with sugar and butter mixture. Boil for 2 minutes, stirring constantly. Cool until lukewarm and add vanilla extract. Beat until creamy and spreadable.

butter nut cake no. 1

1 cup butter
2 cups sugar
1 teaspoon baking soda
1/4 teaspoon salt
1 cup buttermilk

3 cups cake flour, sifted before measuring
3 eggs, separated
3 teaspoons Superior Vanilla, Butter, and Nut Flavoring

Cream butter and sugar thoroughly. Mix baking soda and salt in buttermilk and add to the butter and sugar mixture alternately with flour, mixing well. Add egg yolks one at a time, beating well after each addition. Blend in the flavoring. Beat eggs until stiff peaks form and fold into batter. Pour into greased and floured 10-inch tube pan. Bake at 350°F for 1 hour or until tests done.

butter nut cake no. 2

1 cup vegetable shortening
2 cups sugar
4 eggs
2-1/2 cups cake flour

1 cup milk
1/2 cup self-rising flour
2 teaspoons Superior Vanilla, Butter, and Nut Flavoring

Cream shortening and sugar with electric mixer at high speed for 10 minutes. Add one egg at a time, beating well. Add 1 cup cake flour and mix with electric mixer on low speed for 1 minute. Add remaining flour and milk to batter alternately, mixing well. Add flavoring, mixing well. Pour into two greased and floured 9-inch layer cake pans. Bake at 325°F for 45 minutes or until tests done. Ice with **Butter Nut Icing**.

butter nut icing

1/2 cup butter, softened
8 ounces cream cheese
4 cups confectioners sugar

1 tablespoon Superior Vanilla, Butter, and Nut Flavoring
1 cup chopped pecans

Cream butter and cream cheese well; add confectioners sugar and flavoring, blending well. Stir in pecans.

. . . .

butter pecan cake

3 tablespoons butter
1 cup chopped pecans, toasted
2/3 cup butter, softened
1-1/3 cups sugar
2 eggs

2 cups flour
1-1/2 teaspoons baking powder
1/4 teaspoon salt
2/3 cup milk
1-1/2 teaspoons vanilla extract

Melt 3 tablespoons butter in a 13 x 9 x 2-inch baking pan. Stir in pecans. Bake at 350°F for 10 minutes. Cool.

Cream butter and sugar until light and fluffy. Add eggs one at a time, beating well after each addition. Combine flour, baking powder, and salt; add to creamed mixture alternately with milk. Stir in vanilla extract and pecans. Pour batter into 2 greased and floured 9-inch layer cake pans. Bake at 350°F for 30 minutes or until cakes test done. Cool completely and spread top and sides of cake with **Butter Pecan Frosting**.

butter pecan frosting

3 tablespoons butter
3 cups confectioners sugar
3 tablespoons plus 1 teaspoon milk

3/4 teaspoon vanilla extract
1/3 cup chopped pecans, toasted

Cream butter; add sugar, milk, and vanilla extract, beating until light and fluffy. Stir in pecans.

. . . .

buttermilk gingerbread

1/2 cup butter
1/2 cup sugar
1 egg
1/2 cup molasses
1-2/3 cups cake flour
1/2 teaspoon baking soda

1/4 teaspoon salt
1/2 teaspoon cinnamon
3/4 teaspoon ground ginger
1/2 teaspoon allspice
1/2 cup plus 2 tablespoons
   buttermilk

Cream butter and sugar until smooth; add egg and beat until smooth and creamy. Add molasses and beat vigorously until well blended. Add sifted dry ingredients to batter alternately with buttermilk.

Line bottom of an 8 x 8 x 2-inch baking pan with waxed paper; grease paper and sides of pan lightly. Pour batter into pan. Bake at 350°F for 25 to 30 minutes. Serve warm with whipped cream or applesauce.

. . . .

caramel pecan cake

2 sticks butter
2 cups sugar
5 eggs
3-1/2 cups cake flour

3 teaspoons baking powder
1/4 teaspoon salt
1 cup milk
1 teaspoon vanilla extract

Cream together butter and sugar until light and fluffy. Add eggs one at a time, beating well after each addition. Add sifted flour, baking powder, and salt to batter alternately with milk and vanilla extract, blending well. Pour batter into three or four greased and floured 9-inch layer cake pans. Bake at 350°F for 25 to 30 minutes or until cakes test done. Spread **Caramel Pecan Icing** between layers and on top and sides of cake.

caramel pecan icing

3 cups sugar
1 cup evaporated milk
1 stick butter
1 teaspoon vanilla extract

1/2 cup sugar
1/2 cup boiling water
1 cup chopped pecans

Combine 3 cups sugar, milk, butter, and vanilla extract in a saucepan and heat to melt butter. Brown 1/2 cup sugar in a heavy skillet until sugar has melted and turned caramel color. Add boiling water slowly and stir well. Pour melted sugar into butter mixture; slowly bring to a boil and cook, stirring occasionally, until it reaches soft ball stage (234°F to 240°F), approximately 8 or 9 minutes. Remove from heat and cool slightly. Add chopped pecans and spread immediately between layers and on top and sides of cake.

carrot pudding cake

1 (18.5-ounce) box yellow cake mix
  (without pudding)
1 (3-3/4-ounce) box instant vanilla
  pudding mix
1/2 teaspoon salt
2 teaspoons cinnamon

4 eggs
1/3 cup milk
1/4 cup Vegetable oil
3 cups shredded carrots
1 cup finely chopped pecans

Combine first 7 ingredients and beat with electric mixer at medium speed approximately 2 minutes. Stir in carrots and pecans. Pour batter into three greased and floured 9-inch layer cake pans. Bake at 350°F for 20 minutes or until tests done. Cool in pans for 10 minutes; remove from pans and cool completely. Spread **Orange Cream Frosting** between layers and on sides and top of cake. Garnish top of cake with pecan halves, if desired.

orange cream frosting

3 tablespoons butter, softened
1 (8-ounce) package cream cheese, softened
1 (16-ounce) box confectioners sugar, sifted
1 tablespoon fresh orange juice
1 tablespoon grated orange zest

Combine butter and cream cheese, beating until light and fluffy. Add confectioners sugar and juice and zest; beat until smooth.

. . . .

carrot walnut cake

1-1/2 cups walnuts
3 cups sifted cake flour
3 teaspoons baking powder
1 teaspoon salt
2 cups firmly packed brown sugar
4 large (or 5 medium) eggs

1 cup vegetable oil
1-1/2 teaspoons cinnamon
1 teaspoon nutmeg
1/4 teaspoon ground cloves
3 tablespoons milk
3 cups grated carrots

Chop 1/2 cup walnuts very fine. Grease three 9-inch layer cake pans well. Sprinkle each with approximately 2-1/2 tablespoons walnuts to coat. Chop remaining walnuts coarsely; set aside. Sift flour, baking powder, and salt together. Combine sugar, eggs, oil, and spices. Beat with electric mixer at high speed until well mixed. Add 1/2 flour mixture; stir until well blended. Add milk, mixing well. Add remaining flour, continuing to mix well. Stir in carrots and walnuts. Pour into cake pans. Bake at 350°F for 25 minutes or until cakes test done. Let stand in pans on wire racks 10 minutes. Turn cakes out onto racks to cool. When cool, frost with a buttercream frosting. Decorate with walnut halves, if desired.

. . . .

carrot orange cake no.1

3-1/2 cups sifted cake flour
2 teaspoons baking powder
1 teaspoon baking soda
1/2 teaspoon salt
1 teaspoon cinnamon
1/2 teaspoon nutmeg
1/2 cup butter, softened

3/4 cup firmly packed brown sugar
3 eggs
1/4 cup fresh orange juice
1 tablespoon grated orange zest
2 cups grated carrots
1 cup chopped pecans

Preheat oven to 350°F. Grease and flour a 10-inch bundt or tube pan. Sift flour, baking powder, baking soda, salt, cinnamon, and nutmeg together. Cream butter and sugar until light and fluffy; add eggs one at a time, beating well after each addition. Add flour to batter alternately with juice, beginning and ending with flour mixture. Stir in zest, carrots, and pecans. Spoon batter into prepared pan. Bake at 350°F for 45 minutes or until tests done. Cool in pan for 10 minutes; turn out onto wire rack; cool completely. Spread with **Cream Cheese Frosting**. Garnish with shredded raw carrot and quartered orange slices, if desired.

cream cheese frosting

1 (8-ounce) package cream cheese, softened
1/2 cup confectioners sugar
1 teaspoon vanilla extract

Beat together all ingredients until light and fluffy.

carrot orange cake no. 2

2 sticks butter, softened
2 cups sugar
1 teaspoon cinnamon
1/2 teaspoon nutmeg

1 tablespoon grated orange zest
4 eggs
3 cups flour
1/2 teaspoon salt

3 teaspoons baking powder
1/3 cup fresh orange juice

1-1/2 cups grated carrots
2/3 cup chopped pecans

Preheat oven to 350°F. Grease and flour tube pan. Cream butter and sugar. Add spices and orange zest. Beat eggs well in a separate bowl. Add to the butter and sugar. Sift flour, salt, and baking powder together and add to batter alternately with orange juice. Fold in carrots and nuts. Bake 1 hour or until tests done. Cool in pan 10 minutes and turn out onto wire rack. Dust with confectioners sugar, if desired, or spread with your favorite cream cheese frosting.

. . . .

carrot pecan cake

1-1/4 cups vegetable oil
2 cups sugar
2 cups flour
2 teaspoons baking powder
1 teaspoon baking soda

1 teaspoon salt
2 teaspoons cinnamon
4 eggs
1 cup finely chopped pecans
2 cups grated carrots

Combine oil and sugar and mix well. Sift all dry ingredients together and beat into oil and sugar mixture alternately with eggs, beating well after each addition. Add carrots and pecans. Pour into a lightly greased tube pan. Bake at 325°F for 1 hour and 10 minutes. Cool in pan. Spread **Orange Glaze** over cake, if desired.

orange glaze

1 cup sugar
1/4 cup cornstarch
1 cup fresh orange juice

2 tablespoons butter
2 tablespoons grated orange peel
1/2 teaspoon salt

Combine sugar and cornstarch in saucepan; add juice slowly and stir until smooth. Stir in butter, orange peel, and salt. Cook over low heat until thick and glossy. Cool and spread over cake.

carrot layer cake

1-1/2 cups vegetable oil
2 cups sugar
4 eggs
2 teaspoons vanilla extract
2 cups sifted flour

2 teaspoons baking soda
1 teaspoon salt
3 teaspoons cinnamon
3 cups carrots, finely grated

Cream oil and sugar until light and fluffy. Add eggs one at a time, beating well after each addition. Blend in vanilla extract. Sift dry ingredients together and add to creamed mixture, blending well. Fold in carrots. Bake in three or four greased 9-inch layer cake pans. Bake at 325°F for approximately 40 minutes. Cool and spread with **Cream Cheese Icing**.

cream cheese icing

1 stick butter
1 (8-ounce) package cream cheese
1 (16-ounce) box confectioners sugar

1 teaspoon vanilla extract
Pinch of salt
1 cup chopped pecans

Beat together butter and cream cheese until well blended. Add sugar, vanilla extract, and salt, blending well. Fold in pecans. Spread between layers and on top and sides of cake.

carrot lemon cakes

1 cup butter, melted
1-1/4 cups sugar
4 eggs
1 cup mashed, cooked carrots
2 cups flour
1 teaspoon baking powder

1-1/2 teaspoons vanilla extract
3/4 teaspoon lemon extract
2-1/4 cups confectioners sugar
1/4 cup milk
1-1/2 teaspoons lemon extract

Cream butter and sugar well. Add eggs one at a time, beating well after each addition. Add carrots, flour, and baking powder. Beat 1 minute. Stir in vanilla extract and 3/4 teaspoon lemon extract. Spoon into a greased l5 x l0 x l-inch jellyroll pan, spreading to edges. Bake at 350°F for 25 minutes. Cool.

Combine confectioners sugar, milk, and 1-1/2 teaspoons lemon extract. Stir until smooth. Pour glaze over cooled cake. Let stand until glaze is firm. Cut into squares.

christmas cake

1/2 cup candied cherries
1-1/2 cups chopped walnuts
1 cup seedless raisins
1 cup currants
1-1/2 cups sultana raisins
1/2 cup mixed candied fruit peel
2 tablespoons finely chopped
   angelica

1-1/2 cups butter
1-1/2 cups sugar
7 eggs
4 cups sifted cake flour
1 teaspoon salt

Several hours before making cake, halve cherries and put all fruits and nuts in a casserole dish. Mix together well with your hands. Cover loosely with aluminum foil and bake—tossing fruit once or twice—at 240°F until fruit is well heated through. Cool.

Cream butter and sugar well. Add eggs one at a time, beating well after each addition. Add flour and salt mixture, mixing well. Separate cooled fruit with fingers and fold into batter.

Bake in 10-inch tube pan oiled and lined with heavy paper. Cover the pan with a tin plate.

Bake at 300°F for 1 hour; reduce to 280°F. Remove tin plate after an additional 2 hours and continue baking for another 3 hours, approximately 6 hours in all. Reduce heat if baking too fast and keep gradually reducing heat. Should be golden brown rather than deep brown on top.

carrot pineapple cake

3 eggs
2 cups sugar
1-1/4 cups vegetable oil
3 cups cake flour
2 teaspoons baking soda
1 teaspoon salt

2 teaspoons cinnamon
1-1/2 cups grated carrots
1 cup chopped pecans
1 (20-ounce) can crushed pineapple, well drained
2 teaspoons vanilla extract

Combine eggs, sugar, and oil, beating well. Sift flour, baking soda, salt, and cinnamon together; add to sugar mixture and beat well. Stir in carrots, pecans, pineapple, and vanilla extract. Pour into a greased and lightly floured 10-inch tube pan. Bake at 350°F for 1 hour and 15 minutes or until tests done. Cool in pan for 10 minutes. Remove from pan and cool completely. Serve plain or with your favorite buttercream frosting.

cherry dessert cake squares

2 eggs
1 cup sugar
1 teaspoon vanilla extract
1-1/4 cups cake flour
1 teaspoon baking powder
1/2 teaspoon salt
1/2 cup chopped pecans

1 (16-ounce) can pitted tart cherries
3/4 cup sugar
2 tablespoons cornstarch
1/2 teaspoon almond extract
Sweetened whipped cream or vanilla ice cream

Beat eggs until thick and lemon-colored; gradually add 1 cup sugar, beating well. Add vanilla extract and blend well. Sift flour, baking powder, and salt together. Add to egg mixture and mix thoroughly. Stir in pecans. Pour 2/3 batter into a greased and floured 9-inch square baking pan, spreading evenly. Drain cherries, reserving juice. Stir cherries into remaining batter. Pour batter evenly over first layer. Bake at 350°F for 45 to 50 minutes. Cool. Cut cake into 3-inch squares.

Add water to cherry juice to equal 1 cup. Combine remaining sugar and corn-starch in a saucepan; stir well. Add cherry juice, stirring well. Cook over low heat until clear and thickened. Stir in almond extract. Spoon cherry topping over each serving. Serve squares with a dollop of whipped cream or a scoop of ice cream.

cherry upside-down cake

1 cup butter, divided
2 cups sugar, divided
1 (16-ounce) can pitted tart cherries, drained
1 cup chopped pecans
2 eggs

2-1/2 cups cake flour
1 tablespoon baking powder
1/4 teaspoon salt
2/3 cup milk
1 teaspoon vanilla extract
Sweetened whipped cream

Melt 1/3 cup butter in a 10-inch cast iron skillet. Spread 1/2 cup sugar evenly over butter; cook over low heat until sugar is dissolved. Arrange cherries and chopped pecans in skillet; remove from heat. Cream remaining 2/3 cup butter; gradually add remaining 1-1/2 cups sugar, beating until light and fluffy. Add eggs one at a time, beating well after each addition.

Sift flour, baking powder, and salt together 3 times. Stir well and add to creamed mixture alternately with milk, beginning and ending with flour mixture. Stir in vanilla extract and blend well. Spoon batter evenly over cherries and pecans in skillet. Bake at 350°F for 50 minutes or until tests done. Cool in skillet 10 minutes, then invert cake onto a cake plate. Cool cake completely. Top with sweetened whipped cream and garnish with cherries and pecan halves, if desired.

cherry layer cake

1 cup butter, softened
1 cups granulated sugar
1 tablespoon kirsch
2 cups cake flour

2 teaspoons baking powder
1/4 teaspoon salt
2/3 cup whole milk
4 large egg whites

In a large mixing bowl, cream butter until smooth. Gradually add sugar, beating thoroughly. Stir in kirsch. Sift flour, baking powder, and salt together. Add to batter alternately with milk beginning and ending with flour mixture. With an electric mixer, beat egg whites until stiff, but not dry. Fold gently into batter. Pour into two greased and floured 9-inch layer cake pans. Bake at 350°F for approximately 25 minutes or until cakes test done. Cool. Frost with **Cherry Seven-Minute Frosting**.

cherry seven-minute frosting

2 large egg whites
1-1/2 cups sugar
1/8 teaspoon salt
1/4 teaspoon cream of tartar
1/3 cup white wine

1 teaspoon pure almond extract
1/2 cup almonds, finely chopped
1/3 cup maraschino cherries, finely
   chopped

Place egg whites, sugar, salt, cream of tartar, and wine in top of double boiler over boiling water.

Beat with an electric mixer constantly for approximately 6 to 7 minutes until mixture is stiff.

Remove from heat and place top of double boiler in a pan of cold water. Beat in almond extract until mixture is stiff and shiny.

Remove approximately 1/3 of the frosting and stir in almonds and cherries. Spread between layers. Frost top and sides with remaining icing.

cherry cake

1 cup butter
1 cup sugar
5 eggs
3-1/2 cups sifted cake flour

1/2 teaspoon baking powder
1 teaspoon grated lemon zest
1-1/2 cups candied cherries
3 tablespoons ground almonds

Cream together butter and sugar until soft and fluffy. Add eggs one at a time, beating well after each addition. Stir in sifted flour and baking powder 1/2 cup at a time, mixing well. Add lemon zest, cherries, and almonds and blend thoroughly. Bake in a greased tube pan or bundt pan at 300°F for 1 hour and 30 minutes or until tests done.

. . . .

chocolate cake

2 sticks butter
2 cups sugar
5 eggs
1 teaspoon vanilla extract

3-1/2 cups cake flour
3 teaspoons baking powder
1/4 teaspoon salt
1 cup milk

Cream together butter and sugar until light and fluffy. Add eggs one at a time, beating well after each addition. Add vanilla extract and blend well. Add sifted dry ingredients to batter alternately with milk. Pour into three greased and floured 9-inch layer cake pans. Bake at 350°F for 20 to 25 minutes or until tests done. Spread **Chocolate Icing** over sides and top and between layers. Decorate with pecans, if desired.

chocolate icing

1-1/2 cups sugar
1/4 cup cocoa
6 tablespoons milk

6 tablespoons butter
1 teaspoon vanilla extract

Combine all ingredients and stir over medium heat until mixture comes to full boil. Cook 1 minute and remove from heat and beat until mixture begins to thicken. Double recipe for a thicker icing.

. . . .

chocolate sheet cake

1 cup butter	1-1/2 teaspoons baking soda
2 cups sugar	2/3 cup buttermilk
4 eggs	2/3 cup boiling water
2 cups cake flour	3 ounces unsweetened chocolate
1/4 teaspoon salt	1 teaspoon vanilla extract

Cream butter and sugar thoroughly; add eggs one at a time, beating well after each addition. Sift together flour and salt twice. Combine soda and buttermilk. Add flour and buttermilk to batter alternately to creamed mixture, beginning and ending with flour. Pour boiling water over chocolate, stirring until smooth. Add to batter. Mix well, add vanilla extract.

Pour into a well-greased and floured 9 x 13-inch pan. Bake at 325°F for 50 minutes to 1 hour.

Frost with your favorite chocolate or fudge frosting.

. . . .

cherry pecan cake

2 cups butter	1/4 pound candied pineapple
2 cups sugar	5 cups chopped pecans
6 egg yolks	2 tablespoons lemon extract
3 cups sifted cake flour	6 egg whites
3/4 pound candied cherries	

Cream butter, add sugar and mix until smooth and light. Add egg yolks one at a time, beating well after each addition. Sift flour over fruit and nuts and toss together until well coated. Stir into butter and egg mixture. Add lemon extract. Beat egg whites stiff but not dry; fold into batter. Pour into a well-greased bundt or tube pan. Bake at 300°F for 1 hour and 45 minutes. Serve plain or with **Lemon Juice Sugar Glaze**.

lemon juice sugar glaze

Juice of 2 freshly squeezed lemons
1-1/2 cups confectioners sugar

Heat lemon juice and add confectioners sugar. Stir until dissolved. Pour over warm cake.

. . . .

chocolate fudge cake

1 cup butter
2 cups sugar
4 eggs
3 cups cake flour
1/2 teaspoon salt

1-1/2 teaspoons baking soda
1 cup buttermilk
1 teaspoon vanilla extract
3 ounces unsweetened chocolate, grated

Preheat oven to 325°F. Cream butter and sugar. Add eggs one at a time, beating well after each addition. After last egg has been added, beat for 1 minute or until mixture is light and fluffy. Sift flour and salt together. Mix baking soda and buttermilk and add to batter alternately with flour to creamed mixture. Add vanilla extract. Melt chocolate in 2/3 cup boiling water; stir until smooth. Blend chocolate into cake mixture. Pour into a greased and floured 9 x 13 x 1-1/2-inch pan. Bake at 325°F for 1 hour or until tests done.

Cool in pan. While cake is still slightly warm, remove from pan and frost with **Chocolate Frosting**.

chocolate frosting

4 ounces unsweetened chocolate
1/2 cup butter
3 cups sifted confectioners sugar

Pinch of salt
1 teaspoon vanilla extract
1/2 to 2/3 cup evaporated milk

Melt chocolate and butter over hot water. Sift sugar and salt together and add vanilla extract and chocolate mixture. Add enough milk to make spreading consistency.

• • • • • • • •

chocolate chip fudge cake

6 ounces butter
6 ounces unsweetened chocolate
6 eggs
3 cups sugar
1/2 teaspoon salt

2 teaspoons vanilla extract
1-1/2 cups flour
1-1/2 cups semi-sweet chocolate
  chips

Melt butter and unsweetened chocolate over low heat. Remove from heat and cool to lukewarm. In a large mixing bowl, beat eggs, sugar, salt, and vanilla extract together just to combine. Blend in butter and chocolate mixture. Stir in flour and chocolate chips, blending well.

Pour into two greased 9-inch round layer cake pans, the bottoms of which are lined with waxed paper. Bake at 350°F for 30 to 40 minutes. Cake will be more cake-like and less fudgy if baked for a longer period of time. Frost with **Elegant Fudge Frosting**.

elegant fudge frosting

1-1/4 cups sugar
2 tablespoons instant coffee
  granules
1 cup heavy cream

5 ounces unsweetened chocolate,
  finely chopped
8 tablespoons butter
1 teaspoon vanilla extract

Combine sugar, instant coffee, and cream in deep saucepan. Bring to a boil, stirring constantly. (Mixture will greatly increase in volume during boiling.) Reduce heat; simmer 6 minutes without stirring. Remove from heat. Add chopped chocolate; stir to blend. Stir in butter and vanilla extract. Chill until mixture begins to thicken. Beat until thick and creamy. Can be rewhipped next day if left to stand and thicken.

chocolate beet cake

2 cups cake flour
2 teaspoons baking powder
1/2 teaspoon salt
1/3 cup cocoa
1/2 cup corn oil
1 cup sugar
3 eggs

1/4 cup orange juice
1 teaspoon vanilla extract
1 cup grated, cooked beets
2 teaspoons grated orange zest
6 ounces semi-sweet chocolate
    morsels
Confectioners sugar (optional)

Sift flour, baking powder, salt, and cocoa together; set aside. Combine oil and sugar and mix thoroughly. Add eggs one at a time, beating well after each addition. Add flour mixture to batter alternately with orange juice and vanilla extract, mixing well. Add beets and orange zest and mix thoroughly. Stir in chocolate morsels.

Pour into a greased 13 x 9 x 2-inch baking pan. Bake at 350°F for 40 minutes or until tests done. Cool 10 minutes in pan. Remove from pan and cool completely on wire rack. Sprinkle with confectioners sugar, if desired.

chocolate coconut cake

2 cups cake flour
2 cups sugar
1 teaspoon baking soda
1 cup water

1/2 cup butter
1/4 cup cocoa
2 eggs
1/2 cup buttermilk

Sift flour, sugar, and soda together in a large mixing bowl. Combine water, butter, and cocoa in a small saucepan; cook over low heat until mixture comes to a boil. Remove from heat and stir into dry ingredients, mixing thoroughly. Stir in eggs and buttermilk, mixing thoroughly.

Spoon batter into a well-greased 13 x 9 x 2-inch pan. Bake at 350°F for 30 minutes or until tests done. Cool. Frost with **Chocolate Coconut Frosting**.

chocolate coconut frosting

1 (16-ounce) box confectioners
  sugar
1 cup chopped pecans
1 cup shredded coconut

1/3 cup plus 2 teaspoons milk
1/2 cup butter
3 tablespoons cocoa

Combine sugar, pecans, and coconut. Combine milk, butter, and cocoa and cook over low heat until mixture comes to a boil. Add chocolate mixture to sugar mixture and beat with electric mixer until frosting is light and fluffy.

. . . .

chocolate marble cake

3 cups sifted cake flour
3 teaspoons baking powder
1/2 teaspoon salt
3/4 cup butter
2 cups sugar
3 /4 cup milk
1 teaspoon vanilla extract

6 egg whites, stiffly beaten
9 ounces unsweetened chocolate,
  melted
4 tablespoons sugar
1/4 cup boiling water
1/4 teaspoon baking soda

Sift flour once, measure; add baking powder and salt to flour, and sift together 3 times. Cream butter thoroughly; add sugar gradually and cream together until light and fluffy. Add flour to batter alternately with milk, a small amount at a time; beating well after each addition until smooth. Add vanilla extract. Fold in egg whites. To melted chocolate, add sugar and boiling water, stirring until blended. Add baking soda and stir until thickened. Cool slightly. Divide batter into 2 parts. To 1 part add chocolate mixture. Put by tablespoons into greased pan, 10 x 10 x 2-inch, alternating light and dark mixtures. Bake at 350°F for 55 minutes or until tests done. Spread **Chocolate Seven-Minute Frosting** on top and sides of cake.

chocolate seven-minute frosting

2 egg whites
1/4 teaspoon cream of tartar
Pinch of salt
4 or 5 tablespoons cold water
1-1/2 cups sugar

1 teaspoon vanilla extract
3 teaspoons white corn syrup
1 square unsweetened chocolate, melted

Put first 5 ingredients in top of double boiler, then place over boiling water. Beat with electric mixer approximately 4 or 5 minutes until stiff peaks form. Add vanilla extract and syrup and beat until shiny peaks form. Fold in chocolate gently. Spread on cake immediately.

. . . .

chocolate coca-cola® cake

2 sticks butter
2-1/2 tablespoons cocoa
1/2 cup vegetable oil
1/2 cup miniature marshmallows
1 teaspoon baking soda
2 eggs

1 cup Coca-Cola®
2 cups flour
2 cups sugar
1/2 cup buttermilk
1 teaspoon vanilla extract

Combine butter, cocoa, oil, and cola and bring to a boil. Add remaining ingredients in order named; beat well. Pour into a large greased and floured sheet cake pan. Bake at 350°F for 45 minutes. Spread **Coca-Cola® Icing** over warm cake.

coca-cola® icing

6 tablespoons Coca-Cola®
2-1/2 tablespoons cocoa
1 cup chopped pecans
1 stick butter

1 (16-ounce) box confectioners
  sugar
1 teaspoon vanilla extract

Bring first 3 ingredients to a boil; add remaining ingredients and beat until smooth.
Spread over warm cake.

. . . .

chocolate cream brownie cakes

1 (4-ounce) package German
  chocolate
5 tablespoons butter
1 (3-ounce) package cream cheese
1/4 cup sugar
1 egg
1 tablespoon flour
1/2 teaspoon vanilla extract

2 eggs
3/4 cup sugar
1/2 teaspoon baking powder
1/4 teaspoon salt
1/2 cup flour
1/2 cup chopped pecans
1 teaspoon vanilla extract

Melt chocolate and 3 tablespoons butter over low heat, stirring constantly. Cool.
Blend remaining butter and cheese until softened. Gradually add 1/4 cup sugar,
beating well. Blend in 1 egg, 1 tablespoon flour, and 1/2 teaspoon vanilla extract;
set aside. Beat 2 eggs until thick and light in color. Gradually add 3/4 cup sugar,
beating until thickened. Add baking powder, salt, and 1/2 cup flour. Blend in
cooled chocolate mixture, nuts, 1 teaspoon vanilla extract. Spread 1/2 of the
chocolate batter in a greased 9-inch square pan. Add cream cheese mixture, spreading evenly. Top with remaining chocolate batter by tablespoons. Drag the tip of a
spatula through batter in a zigzag pattern to marbleize. Bake at 350°F for 35 to 40
minutes. Cool. Cut into serving pieces, as desired.

chocolate marble loaf cake

1/3 cup shortening
1 cup sugar
1 teaspoon vanilla extract
1-1/2 cups sifted cake flour
2 teaspoons baking powder
1/4 teaspoon salt

2/3 cup milk
3 egg whites, stifly beaten
1 ounce unsweetened chocolate, melted
1 tablespoon hot water
1/4 teaspoon baking soda

Cream shortening and sugar together until light and fluffy.

Add vanilla extract. Sift flour, baking powder, and salt together 3 times. Add to creamed mixture alternately with milk. Beat until smooth. Fold in egg whites. Combine chocolate, water, and baking soda. Add to 1/2 the batter. Alternate light and dark batter by tablespoons into wax paper-lined 10 x 5 x 3-inch loaf pan. Bake at 300°F for approximately 1 hour. Cool and frost with **Chocolate Frosting**.

chocolate frosting

1/2 cup milk
1/2 teaspoon vanilla extract
2 cups sifted confectioners sugar
2 tablespoons butter
2 ounces unsweetened chocolate, melted

Combine all ingredients in mixer and beat until smooth. Spread on **Chocolate Marble Loaf Cake**.

chocolate spice cake

1/2 cup butter, softened	1 teaspoon cinnamon
1-1/2 cups sugar	2 tablespoons cocoa
3 eggs, separated	3/4 cup buttermilk
1-3/4 cups flour	1 teaspoon vanilla extract
3/4 teaspoon baking powder	1 cup chopped pecans
3/4 teaspoon baking soda	1 teaspoon lemon extract
3/4 teaspoon nutmeg	

Cream butter well; add sugar and beat until light and fluffy. Add egg yolks one at a time, beating well after each addition. Sift all dry ingredients together twice. Add to batter alternately with buttermilk, blending well. Add extracts and pecans. Beat egg whites until stiff but not dry and fold into batter. Pour batter into three greased and floured 9-inch layer cake pans. Bake at 350°F for 25 to 30 minutes or until tests done. Cool completely and frost with your favorite chocolate frosting.

. . . .

chocolate meringue cake

2 cups flour	1/2 cup butter
1 tablespoon baking powder	1 teaspoon vanilla extract
1/4 teaspoon salt	3/4 cup milk
4 eggs, separated	2 ounces semi-sweet chocolate,
2 cups sugar, divided	melted with 3 tablespoons water
1 cup finely chopped pecans	8 pecan halves
1 ounce unsweetened chocolate, grated	

Grease 10-inch tube pan. Line bottom with wax paper; set aside. Sift flour, baking powder, and salt together; set aside. Beat egg whites until soft peaks form. Gradually beat in 1 cup sugar until stiff, glossy peaks form. Fold in pecans and grated chocolate. Spread mixture on bottom and 3/4 up sides of pan. Cream butter and remaining 1 cup sugar until light and fluffy. Beat in egg yolks and vanilla extract until well blended.

Stir in flour mixture alternately with milk until well blended. Pour cake mixture into pan, making sure it is surrounded by meringue on all sides and is lower than the top of meringue. Bake at 325°F for 65 to 70 minutes or until tests done. Do not invert pan. Cool on wire rack 25 minutes or until sides can be loosened easily with metal spatula. Turn out onto cake plate. Peel off wax paper; cool completely. Drizzle with melted chocolate mixture and top with pecans dipped in chocolate mixture.

chocolate strawberry cake

1 (4-ounce) package German
  chocolate
1/2 cup water
1 cup butter
2 cups sugar
4 eggs, separated

1 teaspoon vanilla extract
3 cups sifted cake flour
1/2 teaspoon salt
1 teaspoon baking soda
1 cup buttermilk

Melt chocolate in boiling water and cool. Cream butter and sugar until light and fluffy. Add egg yolks one at a time, beating well after each addition. Blend in melted chocolate and vanilla extract. Add sifted dry ingredients to batter alternately with buttermilk until well blended. Fold in stiffly beaten egg whites. Pour into two greased 9-inch layer cake pans, the bottoms of which have been lined with wax paper. Bake at 350°F for 25 to 30 minutes. Cool completely and spread with **Strawberry Cream Frosting**.

strawberry cream frosting

1 cup heavy cream
3 tablespoons sugar
1 pint fresh strawberries

Whip cream until thickened; add sugar gradually until well blended. Spread 1/2 the cream and 1/2 the strawberries on 1 layer and spread top with the remaining cream and strawberries.

chocolate orange cake

3 cups cake flour	2 cups sugar
3 teaspoons baking powder	4 eggs
3/4 cup Dutch-process cocoa	1-1/2 cups milk
1 pound sweet butter	Grated zest of 4 large oranges

Sift dry ingredients together; set aside. Cream butter until fluffy; add sugar gradually, beating well. Add eggs one at a time, beating well after each addition. Add dry ingredients to batter alternately with milk, blending well. Stir in orange zest. Pour into three greased and floured 9-inch layer cake pans. Bake at 350°F for 25 to 30 minutes. Frost with your favorite chocolate icing.

chocolate mayonnaise cake

2 cups flour	Pinch of salt
1/2 cup cocoa	1 cup water
1 cup sugar	1 cup mayonnaise
1 teaspoon baking soda	1-1/2 teaspoons vanilla extract

Combine flour, cocoa, sugar, baking soda, and salt and mix well. Add water, mayonnaise, and vanilla extract and stir until smooth. Pour batter into a greased and floured 9-inch pan. Bake at 350°F for 25 to 30 minutes or until tests done. Cool completely and spread with **Chocolate Frosting**.

chocolate frosting

2-3/4 cups sifted confectioners sugar
1/4 cup butter, melted
2 tablespoons milk
1/8 teaspoon salt
1/4 cup cocoa
2 egg yolks
1 teaspoon vanilla extract

Combine all ingredients; beat until smooth. Spread on cake immediately.

. . . .

ambassador chocolate cake

2 cups sifted cake flour
1 teaspoon baking soda
1/2 teaspoon salt
1 cup butter
1-1/2 cups firmly packed brown
    sugar

3 eggs, well beaten
4 (1-ounce) squares unsweetened
    chocolate, melted
2/3 cup water

Sift flour once, measure; add baking soda and salt and sift together 3 times. Cream butter thoroughly, add sugar gradually and cream together until light and fluffy. Add eggs and beat well. Add chocolate and beat well. Add flour to batter alternately with water, a small amount at a time, beating well after each addition until smooth. Bake in two greased 9-inch layer cake pans at 350°F for 30 minutes. Spread **Seven-Minute Frosting** between layers and on top and sides of cake, piling frosting thickly on top. When frosting is set, melt 2 additional squares of unsweetened chocolate with 2 teaspoons butter. Pour chocolate over cake.

seven-minute frosting

2 egg whites
1/4 teaspoon cream of tartar
Pinch of salt
1-1/2 cups sugar

5 tablespoons cold water
1 teaspoon vanilla extract
3 teaspoons white corn syrup

Put first 5 ingredients in double boiler over boiling water. Beat with rotary beater 7 minutes or with electric mixer 4 minutes or until icing stands in stiff peaks. Remove from heat. Change hot water in bottom of double boiler for cold and return to heat, return top pan to the double boiler. Add vanilla extract and syrup, beating until icing forms stiff peaks. Spread on cake immediately.

chocolate viennese layer cake

1-3/4 cups sifted cake flour
1 teaspoon salt
2 teaspoons baking powder
1-1/2 cups sugar
1/2 cup butter

1-1/4 cups whipping cream
2 eggs
1 teaspoon vanilla extract
2 (1-ounce) squares unsweetened
    chocolate, melted and cooled

Preheat oven to 350°F. Grease and lightly flour two 9-inch layer cake pans.

Sift flour, salt, baking powder, and sugar together. Cream butter, sift in flour mixture. Mix in 1 cup cream, beat very well. Add eggs, vanilla extract, chocolate, and remaining cream. Beat very well. Divide batter evenly between two prepared pans. Bake 25 minutes or until tests done. Cool on a wire rack for 10 minutes before removing from pans. Cool thoroughly before frosting with **Rich Chocolate Frosting**.

rich chocolate frosting

4 ounces cream cheese
2 tablespoons heavy cream
2 cups confectioners sugar

3 (1-ounce) squares unsweetened
   chocolate, melted
1 teaspoon vanilla extract

Combine all ingredients, mixing well. Spread on cake immediately.

chocolate tea cakes

5 ounces unsweetened chocolate
2/3 cup butter
5 eggs
2-1/2 cups sugar

2 teaspoons vanilla extract
1/2 teaspoon salt
1-1/4 cups cake flour
1-1/2 cups chopped pecans

Combine chocolate and butter in a saucepan over low heat; cook until chocolate and butter melt; set aside. Combine eggs, sugar, vanilla extract, and salt; beat until well blended. Stir in flour, chopped pecans, and chocolate mixture. Pour batter into a lightly greased 15 x 10 x 1-inch jellyroll pan. Bake at 350°F for 25 minutes or until tests done. Cool and frost with **Chocolate Frosting** while still warm. Cut into squares; top each square with a pecan half.

chocolate frosting

1/4 cup plus 2 tablespoons butter
1-1/2 ounces unsweetened
   chocolate, melted

3 tablespoons half-and-half
3 cups sifted confectioners sugar
2 tablespoons whipping cream

Combine first 3 ingredients in saucepan; cook until butter and chocolate melt. Remove from heat and stir in sugar and whipping cream until well blended.

rich chocolate cake

2-1/2 cups sifted cake flour
1/2 teaspoon salt
1 teaspoon baking soda
4 ounces sweet chocolate
1/2 cup brewed coffee

1 cup butter
1-3/4 cups sugar
4 egg yolks
1 cup buttermilk
4 egg whites, stiffly beaten

Sift flour, salt, and baking soda together. Combine chocolate and coffee in top of a double boiler; place over hot water until melted. Cool. Cream butter; gradually beat in sugar until light and fluffy. Add 1 egg yolk at a time, beating well after each addition. Mix in melted chocolate. Add flour mixture to batter alternately with buttermilk, beating until smooth after each addition. Fold in egg whites. Pour into three greased and floured 9-inch layer cake pans. Bake at 350°F for 35 minutes or until tests done. Cool 20 minutes on wire rack. Frost with **Seven-Minute Frosting**, **Cream Cheese Frosting**, or sweetened whipped cream.

· · · · · · · ·

german chocolate cake

1 (4-ounce) package German
    chocolate
1/2 cup water
1 cup butter
2 cups sugar
4 eggs, separated

1 teaspoon vanilla extract
1 teaspoon baking soda
3 cups sifted cake flour
1/2 teaspoon salt
1 cup buttermilk

Melt chocolate in 1/2 cup boiling water and cool. Cream butter and sugar gradually until light and fluffy. Add egg yolks one at a time, beating well after each addition. Blend in melted chocolate and vanilla extract. Add sifted dry ingredients to batter alternately with buttermilk. Fold in stiffly beaten egg whites and pour into three greased and floured 9-inch layer cake pans. Bake at 350°F for 25 to 30 minutes or until tests done. Frost with **Coconut Pecan Frosting**.

coconut pecan frosting

1-1/3 cups evaporated milk
1-1/3 cups sugar
4 egg yolks
2/3 cup butter
1-1/2 teaspoons vanilla extract
1-1/3 cups grated coconut
1-1/3 cups chopped pecans

Combine milk, sugar, egg yolks, and butter in heavy saucepan; bring to a boil and cook over medium heat for 12 minutes, stirring constantly. Add vanilla extract, coconut, and pecans; stir until frosting is cool and spreading consistency.

white chocolate layer cake

1 cup butter
2 cups sugar
4 eggs
4 ounces white chocolate, melted in
  1/2 cup boiling water
3 cups cake flour
1 teaspoon baking soda
1 cup buttermilk
1 teaspoon vanilla extract

Cream butter and sugar until light and fluffy. Add eggs one at a time, beating well after each addition. Cool melted chocolate in water and add to egg mixture. Add sifted dry ingredients to batter alternately with buttermilk. Stir in vanilla extract. Pour into three well-greased and floured 9-inch layer cake pans. Bake at 350°F for 30 minutes or until tests done.

You may vary by folding in egg whites; then folding in 1 cup finely chopped pecans, and 1 cup grated coconut.

Frost with your favorite chocolate or coconut icing.

sour cream devil's food cake

2 cups sifted cake flour
1 teaspoon baking soda
1/2 teaspoon salt
1/3 cup butter
1-1/4 cups sugar
1 egg

3 (1-ounce) squares unsweetened
  chocolate, melted
1 teaspoon vanilla extract
1/2 cup sour cream
3/4 cup whole milk

Sift flour once and measure, add baking soda and salt and sift together 3 times. Cream butter thoroughly, add sugar gradually and cream together well. Add egg and beat thoroughly, then add chocolate and vanilla extract and blend. Add approximately 1/4 of the flour and beat well; then add sour cream and beat thoroughly. Add remaining flour to batter alternately with milk, in small amounts, beating well after each addition. Pour into two greased 9-inch layer cake pans. Bake at 350°F for 30 minutes, or until tests done. Spread **Chocolate Butter Frosting** between layers and on top of cake.

chocolate butter frosting

1 stick butter, melted
4 tablespoons cocoa
6 tablespoons milk
1 teaspoon vanilla extract

1 (16-ounce) box confectioners
  sugar
Chopped pecans, optional

Blend together all ingredients well with an electric mixer. Spread on cake immediately.

. . . .

cocoa cake

2 cups flour
2 cups sugar
3/4 cup Dutch-process cocoa
2 teaspoons baking soda
1 teaspoon baking powder

1/2 cup butter, melted
1 egg
1 cup boiling water
1 cup milk

Preheat oven to 350°F. Sift dry ingredients together. Add remaining ingredients and beat with an electric mixer on medium speed for 2 minutes. Pour into a greased and lightly floured bundt or tube pan. Bake at 350°F for approximately 35 minutes.

Serve plain, dusted with confectioners sugar, or spread with sweetened whipped cream.

. . . .

devil's food cake

2-1/2 cups flour
1 teaspoon baking soda
1 teaspoon baking powder
1/2 cup cocoa
Pinch of salt

2 sticks butter
2 cups sugar
5 eggs
1 cup buttermilk
1 teaspoon vanilla extract

Sift flour, baking soda, baking powder, cocoa, and salt together 3 times. Cream together butter and sugar until light and fluffy. Add eggs one at a time, beating well after each addition. Add flour mixture to batter alternately with buttermilk, blending well after each mixture. Stir in vanilla extract. Pour into three greased and floured 9-inch layer cake pans. Bake at 350°F for 25 minutes. Frost with **Chocolate Icing**, **Seven-Minute Icing**, or **Creole Icing**.

chocolate icing

3 cups sugar
1/2 teaspoon salt
13 large marshmallows, cut up
1 cup evaporated milk

1/2 stick butter
3 ounces unsweetened chocolate
1 teaspoon vanilla extract

Cook sugar, salt, marshmallows, and milk approximately 5 minutes, stirring constantly. Add butter and chocolate and stir until melted. Beat until cool. Add vanilla extract and blend well. If icing is too thick to spread, add a little cream or milk.

creole icing

1/4 cup white corn syrup
1-1/2 cups light brown sugar
3/4 cup sugar
1 cup water

4 egg whites
1/4 teaspoon salt
1 tablespoon vanilla extract
Chopped pecans

Combine syrup, sugars, and water and stir until dissolved. In a medium saucepan, bring mixture to a boil, stirring constantly. Cook, without stirring, until mixture spins a thread. Beat egg whites and salt until stiff but not dry. Pour syrup over egg whites in a very thin stream, beating constantly, until thick enough to spread. Add vanilla extract. Sprinkle finely chopped pecans on top of frosted cake, if desired.

chocolate pudding cake

3/4 cup sugar
1-1/4 cups cake flour
2 tablespoons cocoa
2 teaspoons baking powder
1/4 teaspoon salt
1/2 cup milk
3 tablespoons butter

1 teaspoon vanilla extract
1/2 cup sugar
1/2 cup firmly packed brown sugar
1/4 cup cocoa
1-1/2 cups water
1 cup sweetened whipped cream,
   optional

Sift 3/4 cup sugar, flour, 2 tablespoons cocoa, baking powder, and salt into a 9-inch square pan. Stir in milk, butter, and vanilla extract, and spread mixture evenly in pan.

Combine 1/2 cup sugar, brown sugar, and 1/4 cup cocoa and sprinkle over batter. Slowly pour water over top of pudding. Do not stir. Bake at 350°F for 40 minutes. Serve with sweetened whipped cream, if desired.

congo bars

2/3 cup butter or margarine, melted
1 (16-ounce) box light brown sugar
3 eggs
2-2/3 cups sifted flour

2-1/2 teaspoons baking powder
1/2 teaspoon salt
1 cup chocolate chips
1 cup chopped pecans

Blend butter and sugar. Lightly beat eggs and then beat into mixture. Add flour, baking powder, and salt, mixing well. Add chocolate chips and pecans. Pour into a lightly greased glass baking dish. Bake at 350°F for approximately 45 to 50 minutes. Cut into bars when cooled.

chocolate candy cake

8 (1.55-ounce) milk chocolate
Hershey® bars
2 (6-ounce) cans chocolate syrup
2 teaspoons vanilla extract
2 sticks butter
2 cups sugar

5 eggs
1/2 teaspoon baking soda
2-1/2 cups cake flour
1 cup buttermilk
1 cup chopped pecans

Preheat oven to 350°F. Melt chocolate and syrup in double boiler. Add vanilla extract and cool. Cream butter and sugar until light and fluffy. Add eggs one at a time, beating well after each addition. Add chocolate mixture and beat well. Sift baking soda and flour together twice; add to batter alternately with buttermilk to batter and continue to beat until well blended. Add pecans. Pour into 10-inch tube pan. Bake at 350°F for 1 hour to 1 hour and 30 minutes or until tests done.

Use your favorite chocolate icing and top with pecan halves, if desired.

. . . .

chocolate chiffon cake

1/2 cup cocoa
3/4 cup boiling water
1-3/4 cups flour
1-3/4 cup sugar
1-1/2 teaspoon baking soda

1 teaspoon salt
1/2 cup vegetable oil
8 eggs, separated
2 teaspoons vanilla extract
1/2 teaspoon cream of tartar

Mix cocoa and boiling water and set aside to cool. Sift flour, sugar, baking soda, and salt together. Make a well in the center of the dry ingredients. Add oil, egg yolks, vanilla extract, and cocoa mixture. Beat well, approximately 3 minutes. Beat egg whites and cream of tartar until stiff. Fold into batter. Pour into ungreased 10-inch tube pan. Cut through batter around the post with spatula so that air can escape, preventing a crust from forming on top of the cake. Bake at 325°F for 55 minutes, then increase temperature to 350°F and bake 10 minutes or until tests done. Frost with your favorite chocolate frosting.

milk chocolate cake

8 (1-7/8-ounce) chocolate-covered
  malt-caramel candy bars (Milky
  Way®, for example)
1/2 cup butter, melted
1/2 cup butter, softened
2 cups sugar

4 eggs
1-1/2 teaspoons vanilla extract
1-1/4 cups buttermilk
1/2 teaspoon baking soda
3 cups cake flour
1 cup chopped pecans

Combine candy bars and 1/2 cup melted butter in a saucepan; place over low heat until candy bars are melted, stirring constantly. Cool.

Cream 1/2 cup butter, gradually adding sugar and beat until light and fluffy. Add eggs one at a time, beating well after each addition; stir in vanilla extract.

Combine buttermilk and soda; add to creamed mixture alternately with flour, beating well after each addition; stir in candy bar mixture and pecans.

Pour batter into a greased and floured 10-inch tube pan. Bake at 325°F for 1 hour and 20 minutes or until tests done.

Let cool in pan for 1 hour; remove and completely cool, then frost with **Milk Chocolate Frosting**.

milk chocolate frosting

2-1/2 cups sugar
1 cup evaporated milk
1/2 cup butter, melted

1 (6-ounce) package semi-sweet
  chocolate chips
1 cup marshmallow cream

Combine sugar, milk, and butter in heavy saucepan; cook over medium heat until a small amount dropped in cold water forms a soft ball (234°F to 240°F).

Remove from heat; add chocolate chips and marshmallow cream, stirring until melted.

If necessary, add a small amount of milk to make spreading consistency.

chocolate cream cake

4 eggs
2 cups whipping cream
2 teaspoons vanilla extract
2-1/2 cups sifted cake flour

2 cups sugar
1/2 cup cocoa
3 teaspoons baking powder
1/2 teaspoon salt

Using an electric mixer on medium speed, beat eggs thoroughly, approximately 5 minutes. Gradually beat in cream and vanilla extract, mixing well. Sift flour, sugar, cocoa, baking powder, and salt. Add to egg mixture; beat until smooth. Pour into two greased 9 x 5 x 3-inch loaf pans.

Bake at 350°F for 45 minutes. Cool 10 minutes. Remove from pans. Dust with confectioners sugar. Cool on wire racks. Serve with sweetened strawberries and sweetened whipped cream, if desired.

chocolate sauerkraut cake

1-1/2 cups sugar
2/3 cup butter
3 eggs
1-1/4 teaspoons vanilla extract
2-1/2 cups cake flour
1/4 teaspoon salt

1 teaspoon baking soda
1 teaspoon baking powder
1/2 cup cocoa
1 cup buttermilk
2/3 cup sauerkraut, chopped, rinsed, and drained

Cream together sugar and butter until light and fluffy. Add eggs one at a time, beating well after each addition. Add vanilla extract and blend well. Sift flour, salt, baking soda, baking powder, and cocoa together. Add flour mixture to batter alternately with buttermilk. Fold in sauerkraut. Bake in either a greased and floured sheet cake pan or in two 9-inch layer cake pans at 350°F for 25 to 30 minutes or until tests done. Frost with either **Cream Cheese** or **Mocha Cream Frostings**.

cream cheese frosting

1 (8-ounce) package cream cheese
1 (16-ounce) box confectioners sugar
Milk to soften

Combine all ingredients, blending until soft and creamy.

mocha cream frosting

1 (8-ounce) package cream cheese
1 (16-ounce) box confectioners sugar
2 tablespoons strong brewed coffee

Combine all ingredients, blending until soft and creamy.

. . . .

coconut cream cake

1/2 pound butter
3 cups sugar
6 eggs
3 cups cake flour

1 cup whipping cream
2 teaspoons vanilla extract
1 teaspoon lemon extract

Cream butter and sugar until light and fluffy. Add eggs one at a time, beating well after each addition. Add small amounts of sifted flour to batter alternately with whipping cream and flavorings. Pour into three greased and floured 9-inch layer cake pans. Bake at 350°F for approximately 25 minutes or until tests done. Cool. Frost with **Coconut Cream Frosting**.

coconut cream frosting

4 tablespoons butter
2 cups shredded coconut
1 (8-ounce) package cream cheese

3-1/2 cups confectioners sugar
2 tablespoons milk
1/2 teaspoon vanilla extract

Melt 2 tablespoons butter in skillet; add coconut, stirring constantly until golden brown. Spread coconut on paper towel to cool. Cream remaining butter with cream cheese; add sugar and milk alternately, beating well. Add vanilla extract. Stir in 1-1/4 cups coconut. Spread between layers and on top and sides of cake. Sprinkle remaining coconut over top of cake. Add chopped pecans, if desired.

. . . .

coconut buttermilk cake

1 cup butter, softened
2 cups granulated sugar
6 large eggs, separated
1 teaspoon vanilla extract
3 cups cake flour

1 teaspoon baking soda
1/8 teaspoon salt
1 cup buttermilk
2/3 cup coconut, freshly grated

In a large mixing bowl, cream butter and sugar until light and fluffy. Add egg yolks one at a time, beating well after each addition. Stir in flavoring. Sift flour, baking soda, and salt together, add to batter alternately with buttermilk, beginning and ending with flour mixture. Stir in coconut. Beat egg whites until stiff but not dry. Gently fold into batter. Pour into three or four greased and floured 9-inch layer cake pans. Bake at 350°F for approximately 25 minutes or until cakes test done. Cool in pans on wire racks for approximately 5 minutes before removing from pans. Cool completely, then frost with **Sour Cream Coconut Frosting**.

sour cream coconut frosting

1 (16-ounce) carton sour cream
4 cups coconut, freshly grated
I cup granulated sugar

Combine all ingredients, mixing thoroughly. Spread frosting between layers and on sides and top of cake.

. . . .

coconut marble cake

1 cup butter
2 cups sugar
4 eggs
3 cups cake flour
2 teaspoons baking powder

1 teaspoon salt
1 cup milk
1 teaspoon vanilla extract
1/2 cup chocolate malted milk powder

Cream butter and sugar until soft and fluffy. Add eggs one at a time, beating well after each addition. Sift flour, baking powder, and salt together, add to batter alternately with milk, beating well. Stir in vanilla extract, blending well. Pour 1/2 of the batter into a bowl; blend in malted milk powder, mixing until smooth.

Spoon plain and malted batters alternately into well-greased and floured 10-inch bundt or tube pan. Bake at 350°F for 1 hour to 1 hour and 10 minutes or until tests done. Remove from oven and cool in pan on wire rack for 15 minutes. Invert onto ovenproof cake plate and cool completely. Spread with **Broiled Coconut Frosting**. Bake at 500°F for 2 to 5 minutes, until frosting browns lightly.

broiled coconut frosting

1/4 cup butter
1/2 cup firmly packed brown sugar

1 cup chopped or flaked coconut
1/4 cup heavy cream

Melt butter; while butter is still warm, add brown sugar, coconut, and cream, and stir until sugar is partially melted and mixture is well combined. Spread evenly over cake. Bake at 500°F for 2 to 5 minutes or until frosting is lightly browned.

. . . .

coconut cake

3/4 cup butter
2 cups sugar
6 egg yolks
3 cups sifted cake flour
3 teaspoons baking powder

1 cup milk
3 egg whites
Pinch of salt
1 teaspoon vanilla extract

Cream butter and sugar until light and fluffy. Add egg yolks one at a time, beating well after each addition. Sift flour and baking powder together; add to batter alternately with milk. Beat egg whites and salt until stiff peaks form; fold into batter. Add vanilla extract. Bake at 350°F for 30 minutes or until tests done. Frost with **Coconut Frosting** or **Old Fashioned Coconut Icing**.

coconut frosting

2 cups sugar
1 cup water
1/4 cup light corn syrup
3 egg whites
Pinch of salt

1 teaspoon vanilla extract
Meat of 2 coconuts, grated; or 2 (12-ounce) packages frozen grated coconut

Boil sugar, water, and corn syrup until it spins a thread. Beat egg whites and salt until stiff peaks form. Gradually add hot syrup, beating constantly. Add vanilla extract and cool until spreading consistency. Frost between and on top of layers and sprinkle with coconut, or add the coconut to the frosting and spread evenly over cake.

old fashioned coconut icing
Cook in 2 saucepans; begin the first 10 minutes before the second

First saucepan:
1-1/2 cups sugar
2 cups canned coconut milk or milk of 2 coconuts and water to equal 2 cups
2 handfuls fresh grated coconut

Cook until it begins to thicken; add coconut and cook 1 minute.

Second saucepan:

2 egg whites
1 cup sugar plus 3 tablespoons water

1/2 teaspoon cream of tartar
Pinch of salt
1 teaspoon vanilla extract

Cook all ingredients over hot water, beating constantly for 3 minutes until it stands in peaks.

Put 1 cake layer on a serving dish and spoon some coconut milk and coconut mixture from first saucepan over it. Frost cake layer with frosting from second saucepan, if desired. Continue stacking layers the same way, then cover tops and side of cake with white frosting from second saucepan; cover frosted cake with grated coconut.

cranberry orange cake

1 cup dates, chopped
1 cup chopped walnuts
1 cup cranberries, halved
1/2 cup sifted cake flour
2 cups cake flour
1 teaspoon baking powder
1 teaspoon baking soda
1/4 teaspoon salt

1/2 cup butter
1 cup sugar
2 eggs
2 tablespoons grated orange zest
1 cup buttermilk
2/3 cup orange juice
2/3 cup sugar

Combine dates, walnuts, cranberries, and 1/2 cup flour; set aside. Sift 2 cups flour, baking powder, baking soda, and salt together; set aside.

Cream butter and 1 cup sugar until light and fluffy. Add eggs one at a time, beating well after each addition. Add orange zest and blend well.

Add dry ingredients to batter alternately with buttermilk, beating well after each addition. Stir in fruit and nut mixture. Pour batter into greased 9-inch springform pan.

Bake at 350°F for 1 hour or until tests done. Cool 10 minutes. Remove from pan. Cool on wire rack. Heat orange juice and 2/3 cup sugar until dissolved. Pour over cake.

Let cake stand for 12 hours before slicing.

. . . .

cranberry cake

1 (19-ounce) box lemon cake mix
1 (3-ounce) package cream cheese, softened
3/4 cup milk
4 eggs

1-1/4 cups ground cranberries
1/2 cup ground walnuts
1/4 cup sugar
1 teaspoon mace

Blend cake mix, cream cheese, and milk; beat with mixer for 2 minutes at medium speed. Add eggs one at a time, beating for 2 additional minutes.

Thoroughly combine cranberries, walnuts, sugar, and mace; fold into cake batter.

Pour into a well-greased and floured 10-inch tube pan or bundt pan. Bake at 350°F for 1 hour or until tests done. Cool for 5 minutes before removing from pan. Dust with confectioners sugar, if desired.

. . . .

crumb cake

1 cup butter
2 cups dark brown sugar
3-1/2 cups cake flour
2 teaspoons cinnamon
1 teaspoon ground cloves
1/4 teaspoon salt

1 teaspoon baking soda
1 teaspoon baking powder
1 cup buttermilk
2 eggs
1/2 cup chopped pecans
1 teaspoon vanilla extract

Cream sugar and butter until light and fluffy. Add sifted flour, cinnamon, and cloves until a crumbly mixture forms. Reserve 1 cup of mixture. Combine salt, baking soda, and baking powder and add to the batter alternately with buttermilk, beating well after each addition. Add eggs one at a time, beating well after each addition. Add vanilla extract. Fold in pecans. Pour into a well-greased large tube pan. Sprinkle reserved crumbs on top. Bake at 325°F for 50 minutes or until tests done.

. . . .

coconut cake supreme

1 cup butter
2 cups sugar
4 eggs
1/2 teaspoon salt

1 tablespoon vanilla extract
1 teaspoon baking soda
1-1/2 cups buttermilk
3 cups cake flour

Cream butter and sugar; add eggs one at a time, beating well. Add salt and vanilla extract. Stir soda into buttermilk. Add 1/2 cup flour to batter alternately with 1/2 cup buttermilk, ending with flour.

Pour batter into three greased 9-inch layer cake pans, the bottoms of which have been lined with wax paper. Bake at 350°F for 30 minutes, or until tests done. Cool, then spread **Coconut Filling** between layers and on top and sides.

coconut filling

3 cups sugar
1-1/2 cups milk
1/4 pound butter
1 teaspoon vanilla extract
Meat of 1 large coconut, freshly grated; or 2 (6-ounce) packages frozen
   coconut, defrosted

Cook sugar and milk together until it changes color from white to oyster white.
Remove from heat. Add butter, mix well; add vanilla extract, mix well. Stir in
coconut. Cool to lukewarm and spread between layers and on sides and top of cake.

· · · · · · · · ·

coconut pineapple cake

1 cup butter, softened
2 cups sugar
4 eggs
3-1/2 cups cake flour
2 teaspoons baking powder
1 teaspoon salt

1 cup milk
1 teaspoon lemon juice
1 teaspoon vanilla extract
1/2 teaspoon almond extract
1-1/3 cups flaked coconut

Cream butter; gradually add sugar, beating until light and fluffy. Add eggs one at a
time, beating well after each addition.

Sift flour, baking powder, and salt together; add to creamed mixture alternately
with milk, beginning and ending with flour mixture. Beat with electric mixer on
low speed just until blended. Stir in lemon juice and extracts.

Pour batter into three greased and floured 9-inch layer cake pans. Bake at 350°F
for 25 to 30 minutes or until tests done. Cool in pans 10 minutes; remove from pans.

Spread **Pineapple Filling** between warm layers; let cool. Spread top and sides of
cake with **Heavenly Frosting** and sprinkle with coconut.

pineapple filling

3 tablespoons cake flour
1/2 cup sugar
1/8 teaspoon salt
1 (20-ounce) can crushed pineapple, drained
2 tablespoons butter

Combine flour, sugar, and salt in saucepan. Add pineapple and butter. Cook over medium heat, stirring constantly, until thickened.

heavenly frosting

1-1/2 cups sugar
Pinch of salt
1/2 cup water
1 teaspoon distilled white vinegar
3 egg whites

Combine all ingredients except egg whites in a heavy saucepan. Cook over medium heat, stirring constantly, until mixture is clear. Cook without stirring until syrup spins a 4 x 6-inch ribbon.

Beat egg whites until soft peaks form. Continue beating while slowly adding syrup mixture; beat until stiff peaks form and frosting is spreading consistency.

. . . .

cut-a-ribbon cake

Tie a colorful ribbon around the circumference of this cake to be cut by the guest of honor

8 eggs, separated
2 cups sugar
8 teaspoons lemon juice
2 packages unflavored gelatin
1/2 cup cold water
Grated zest of 2 lemons
2 packages ladyfingers
1 cup whipping cream, whipped
Fresh strawberries or peaches

Combine egg yolks, sugar, and lemon juice in top of a double boiler. Cook, stirring constantly, until thickened. Dissolve gelatin in cold water. Remove mixture from stove; add lemon zest and dissolved gelatin. Cool to room temperature. Beat egg whites until stiff peaks form. Fold into cooled mixture.

Line the sides of a springform pan with a solid row of ladyfingers and line the bottom of the same pan with ladyfingers like the spokes of a wheel. Pour in lemon mixture and let set overnight in refrigerator. Remove sides of pan and invert cake on a large plate. Decorate with whipped cream in spaces between ladyfingers (cream may be flavored with a little lemon zest), and fresh strawberries or peaches.

dutch oatmeal cake

Cake:
1-1/2 cups boiling water
1 cup quick-cooking oats, uncooked
1/2 cup vegetable shortening
1 cup firmly packed brown sugar
2 eggs

2 cups cake flour
1 teaspoon baking soda
1 teaspoon cinnamon
1/2 teaspoon salt

Topping:
1/2 cup firmly packed brown sugar
1/2 cup chopped pecans
1/2 cup butter, melted
1/2 teaspoon vanilla extract
1 cup grated coconut

Combine boiling water and oats, stirring well, let cool.

Cream shortening; add sugar and beat until light and fluffy. Add eggs one at a time, beating well after each addition.

Sift flour, baking soda, cinnamon, and salt together and add to creamed mixture, beating well. Stir in oats mixture until blended well.

Pour into a greased and floured 13 x 9 x 2-inch baking pan. Combine remaining ingredients and spoon over batter. Bake at 350°F for 40 minutes or until tests done.

. . . .

daisy cake

2-1/2 cups self-rising flour
1-1/2 cups sugar
1/2 cup shortening
3 whole eggs, lightly beaten
1 cup milk
1 teaspoon vanilla extract

Combine flour and sugar; set aside.

Measure shortening into bowl, mix to soften; sift flour and sugar mixture into creamed mixture. Stir in eggs and 1/4 cup milk until flour and sugar are dampened and beat vigorously for 2 minutes.

Stir in remaining milk and vanilla extract and beat for 30 seconds.

Pour batter into three greased and floured 9-inch round layer cake pans. Bake at 350°F for approximately 15 to 20 minutes or until lightly browned and cake begins to loosen from sides of pan. Spread with your favorite icing.

. . . .

date orange cake

3-1/2 cups cake flour
1/2 teaspoon salt
1 pound candy orange slices,
   chopped
1 (8-ounce) package chopped dates
2 cups chopped pecans
1 (3-1/2-ounce) can flaked coconut

1 cup butter
2 cups sugar
4 eggs
1/2 cup buttermilk
1 teaspoon baking soda
1/2 cup orange juice
1/2 cup confectioners sugar

Combine flour and salt; set aside.

Combine orange slices, dates, pecans, and coconut; stir in 1/2 cup flour mixture; set aside.

Cream butter; gradually add sugar, beating until light and fluffy. Add eggs one at a time, beating well after each addition.

Combine buttermilk and soda, mixing well. Add remaining 3 cups flour mixture alternately with buttermilk to creamed mixture, beginning and ending with flour. Add candy mixture; stir until well blended.

Spoon batter into a greased and floured 10-inch tube pan. Bake at 300°F for 2 hours or until tests done.

Combine orange juice and confectioners sugar. While cake is still hot, punch holes in top of cake using a toothpick and spoon glaze over top. Cool cake before removing from pan.

. . . .

date pecan cake

1 quart chopped pecans
2 (7-ounce) packages dates,
   chopped
1 cup flour

2 teaspoons baking powder
4 eggs
1 cup sugar
1 teaspoon vanilla extract

Chop nuts and cut dates with kitchen scissors. Sift flour and baking powder together. Add pecans and dates to mixture, coating thoroughly.

Beat together eggs, sugar, and vanilla extract. Add egg mixture to nuts and dates mixture and mix well. Bake in lightly greased tube pan at 300°F for 1 hour or until tests done.

. . . .

dream cake

First mixture:
1 cup flour
1/2 cup butter
1/4 teaspoon salt

Mix together and spread in 9-inch square cake pan.

Second mixture:

2 eggs	**1/2 cup coconut**
1 cup brown sugar	**1/2 cup dates, cut up**
1 teaspoon baking powder	**1/2 cup candied cherries**
1 teaspoon vanilla extract	**1 cup chopped pecans**

Mix and pour over first mixture. Bake at 325°F for approximately 40 minutes or until tests done. Spread **Buttercream Icing** or **Lemon Butter Icing** on top, if desired. Cut into squares before serving.

buttercream icing

4 tablespoons butter, softened
2 cups sifted confectioners sugar
3 tablespoons milk
1 teaspoon vanilla extract

Cream butter well, add sugar and milk alternately, a little at a time, stirring until smooth after each addition. Stir in vanilla extract. When smooth, pour over cake and let stand until set before cutting.

lemon butter frosting

4 tablespoons butter, softened
2 cups sifted confectioners sugar
3 tablespoons lemon juice
1 teaspoon white corn syrup

Cream butter, add sugar and juice alternately, a little at a time, stirring until smooth after each addition. Stir in syrup until smooth and shiny. When icing has set, cut cake for serving.

. . . .

dolley madison's layer cake

3/4 cup butter
2-1/2 cups sugar
3 cups cake flour
3/4 cup cornstarch
1 cup milk
2-1/2 teaspoons vanilla extract
8 egg whites, stiffly beaten

Cream butter and sugar together until light and fluffy. Add sifted dry ingredients alternately with milk and vanilla extract. Beat egg whites until stiff peaks form, adding approximately 3 tablespoons sugar. Fold in egg whites gently but thoroughly.

Pour batter into four greased and floured 9-inch round cake pans. Bake at 350°F for 20 to 25 minutes or until tests done. Spread with **Dolley Madison's Caramel Icing**.

dolley madison's caramel icing

3-1/2 cups light brown sugar
1 cup heavy cream
4 tablespoons butter
1 teaspoon vanilla extract

Heat sugar, cream, and butter in a double boiler; cook for approximately 15 to 20 minutes. Add vanilla extract. Spread immediately on cake.

. . . .

dolley madison's pecan cake

1/2 cup butter
1 cup sugar
2 cups cake flour
2 teaspoons baking powder
1 cup milk

1/2 teaspoon vanilla extract
1-1/2 cups chopped pecans
4 egg whites, stiffly beaten
3 tablespoons sugar

Cream together butter and sugar, beating thoroughly; add sifted dry ingredients alternately with milk and vanilla extract. Beat egg whites until soft peaks form; add 3 tablespoons sugar until stiff peaks form. Fold in pecans. Fold in egg whites. Bake in a greased and floured loaf pan at 350°F for approximately 50 minutes.

. . . .

fig cake

1 cup butter
2 cups sugar
3-1/2 cups sifted cake flour
2 teaspoons baking powder

1 teaspoon salt
1 cup milk
1 teaspoon vanilla extract
8 egg whites

Cream butter and sugar together until light and fluffy. Sift dry ingredients together twice; add to creamed mixture alternately with milk. Add vanilla extract. Fold in egg whites beaten stiff but not dry. Pour batter into three greased and floured 9-inch layer cake pans. Bake at 350°F for 20 to 25 minutes. Spread **Fig Filling** between layers of cake and frost sides and top with **Seven-Minute Frosting**.

fig filling

2 cups dried figs
1 cup crushed pineapple
3 cups water
1/4 teaspoon salt
2 cups sugar

Rinse figs in hot water and drain. Clip off stems and cut figs into thin strips. Combine with pineapple and water and cook on medium heat approximately 10 minutes. Add salt and sugar and cook, stirring occasionally, until figs are tender and mixture is very thick, approximately l0 to 15 minutes. Cool. Recipe provides filling for three 9-inch layers.

seven-minute frosting

1-1/2 cups sugar
2 egg whites
1/4 teaspoon salt

1/3 cup water
1/4 teaspoon cream of tartar
1 teaspoon vanilla extract

Combine all ingredients except vanilla extract in top of double boiler. Beat until thoroughly mixed. Place over rapidly boiling water and beat constantly for 7 minutes or until icing will hold a peak. Remove from heat and add vanilla extract. Beat until cool and thick enough to spread. Spread immediately over sides and top of cake.

fig preserves cake

1 cup vegetable oil
2 cups sugar
3 eggs
2 cups flour
1 teaspoon baking soda
1 teaspoon allspice

1 teaspoon cinnamon
1 teaspoon nutmeg
2/3 cup buttermilk
1 cup fig preserves, undrained
1 cup chopped pecans
Confectioners sugar

Combine oil and sugar in large mixing bowl and beat until light and well blended. Add eggs one at a time, beating well after each addition. Add sifted dry ingredients alternately with buttermilk, blending well after each addition. Fold in preserves and pecans thoroughly.

Pour batter into a greased and floured tube pan. Bake at 350°F for 1 hour or until tests done. Dust with confectioners sugar.

. . . .

fruit cocktail cake

2 eggs
1/3 cup evaporated milk
2-1/2 cups cake flour
2 cups sugar

2 teaspoons baking soda
Pinch of salt
1 (17-ounce) can fruit cocktail,
   undrained

Beat together eggs, evaporated milk, flour, sugar, baking soda, salt, and fruit cocktail. Pour into a greased and floured 13 x 9 x 2-inch baking pan. Bake at 350°F for 30 minutes. Cool 30 minutes, then turn out onto serving tray. Spread **Glaze** over top and sides of cake.

glaze

3/4 cup sugar
1/3 cup butter, melted
1/2 cup chopped pecans
1/3 cup evaporated milk
1 teaspoon vanilla extract

Combine all ingredients well and pour over cake while still warm.

. . . .

ginger cakes

3 cups cake flour
1 teaspoon allspice
1 teaspoon baking powder
1 teaspoon cinnamon
1/2 teaspoon ground ginger
1 teaspoon baking soda
1/4 cup butter
1/4 cup lard or vegetable
   shortening

3/4 cup sugar
2 eggs
1/2 cup buttermilk
3/4 cup molasses
1 cup nuts, chopped fine
1/2 pound raisins, chopped

Sift all dry ingredients together; set aside. Beat butter and lard or shortening together; add sugar, beating until light and fluffy. Add eggs one at a time, beating well after each addition. Add dry ingredients and milk and syrup alternately, blending well. Add nuts and raisins, blending well.

Spoon mixture onto a greased cookie sheet for ginger cakes or, to make gingerbread men, add enough flour so that dough can be rolled out and gingerbread men cut out with cookie cutters. Press a few raisins on each cake, if desired. Bake at 350°F for 15 to 20 minutes or until tests done.

. . . .

fruit preserves cake

3 cups sifted cake flour
1 teaspoon baking soda
1/2 teaspoon cinnamon
1/2 teaspoon nutmeg
1/2 teaspoon ground cloves
3/4 cup butter
2 cups firmly packed brown sugar

4 eggs, separated
1 teaspoon vanilla extract
1/2 cup buttermilk
2/3 cup strawberry preserves
2/3 cup pineapple preserves
2/3 cup apricot preserves
1 cup chopped pecans

Sift flour, baking soda, cinnamon, nutmeg, and cloves together; set aside. Cream together butter and brown sugar until light and fluffy. Add egg yolks, beat well. Add vanilla extract. Add dry ingredients to batter alternately with buttermilk, beating well after each addition. Stir in preserves and pecans. Beat egg whites until stiff peaks form and fold into batter.

Pour into greased 10-inch tube pan. Bake in 350°F for 1 hour and 30 minutes or until tests done. Cool 10 minutes in pan and remove. Continue cooling on wire rack.

gingerbread cake

1/4 cup butter
1/4 cup lard or vegetable shortening
1/2 cup sugar
1 egg, beaten
1 cup dark molasses
2-1/2 cups cake flour

1-1/2 teaspoons soda
1/2 teaspoon salt
1/2 teaspoon ground cloves
1 teaspoon ginger
1 teaspoon cinnamon
1 cup hot water

Cream butter, lard or shortening, and sugar; add egg, followed by molasses. Add dry ingredients, and hot water. Beat with electric mixer for several minutes. Pour into a buttered baking dish. Bake at 325°F for approximately 30 minutes. Top with **Applesauce Topping**.

applesauce topping

8 tart apples
Juice of 1 lemon
2 drops red food coloring

Peel apples and cut into little pieces. Combine in a saucepan with lemon juice. Cover and simmer until apples are soft, being careful not to burn apples. Put mixture through a sieve. Add food coloring.

· · · · · · · ·

hawaiian cake

1 cup candied pineapple
1-1/2 cups sifted cake flour
1-1/2 teaspoons baking powder
1/2 cup butter
1 cup sifted confectioners sugar
2 eggs

1 teaspoon vanilla extract
1 cup milk
1/2 cup chopped unsalted
macadamia nuts
1/2 cup flaked coconut

Slice pineapple into small pieces; set aside. Sift flour and baking powder together.
Cream butter and sugar until light and fluffy. Add eggs one at a time, beating well after each addition. Stir in vanilla extract. Add flour mixture alternately with milk, beating just until smooth. Fold in pineapple, nuts, and coconut. Pour into buttered and floured bundt pan. Bake at 350°F for approximately 45 minutes or until tests done. Loosen edges and turn out onto wire rack to cool completely.

· · · · · · · ·

hot milk cake

1 cup milk
1 stick butter
4 eggs, well beaten
2 cups sugar

2 cups sifted flour
2 teaspoons baking powder
1/2 teaspoon salt
1 teaspoon vanilla extract

In small saucepan, bring milk and butter to a boil. In medium mixing bowl, combine other ingredients and mix well. Combine two mixtures and pour into a greased and floured 10-inch tube pan or three greased and floured 8-inch layer cake pans. Bake immediately at 350° F for 35 to 40 minutes in a tube pan or for 25 minutes in layer cake pans, or until tests done. Serve warm or cold, with **Hot Fudge Sauce.**

hot fudge sauce

3 tablespoons cocoa
3/4 cup sugar
2 tablespoons water
Pinch of salt

1 small can evaporated milk
2 tablespoons butter
1 teaspoon vanilla extract

Put all dry ingredients in saucepan and blend until cocoa dissolves. Add milk; bring to gentle boil (3 to 4 minutes), stirring constantly. Do not use high heat. Remove from heat and stir in butter and vanilla extract. Pour over cake or ice cream while sauce in still hot.

graham cracker cake

Cake:
3/4 cup butter
1-1/2 cups sugar
5 eggs, separated
1/2 cup flour
2 teaspoons baking powder

1/4 teaspoon salt
3 cups graham cracker crumbs
1-1/4 cups milk
1 teaspoon vanilla extract

Filling:

1/4 cup cake flour
1 cup sugar
1/2 teaspoon salt

2 cups milk, scalded
2 egg yolks, lightly beaten
1 teaspoon vanilla extract

To prepare cake: Cream butter and sugar until light and fluffy. Add egg yolks, beating well. Sift flour, baking powder, and salt together; combine with graham cracker crumbs. Add to batter alternately with milk, beating well after each addition. Stir in vanilla extract. Beat egg whites until stiff peaks form; fold into batter.

Pour batter into three greased and floured 9-inch layer cake pans. Bake at 350°F for 25 to 30 minutes. Cool completely. Spread filling between layers and **Brown Sugar Frosting** on sides and top of cake.

To prepare filling: Combine flour, sugar, and salt in a saucepan. Slowly stir in milk; cook over low heat for 15 minutes or until thickened, stirring constantly. Add a small amount of the mixture to yolks. Stir yolk mixture into hot mixture. Remove from heat and stir in vanilla extract. Cool and spread between layers of cake.

brown sugar frosting

1 cup firmly packed light brown sugar
1/4 cup water
2 egg whites

Combine sugar and water in a heavy saucepan; cook over low heat to soft ball stage (234°F to 240°F). Beat egg whites until soft peaks form. Continue beating and gradually add syrup mixture; beat well. Frost sides and top of cake.

· · · · · · · · ·

southern special jam cake

1 cup butter
2 cups sugar
3 eggs
3 cups flour
1/2 teaspoon salt
1 teaspoon each cinnamon, nutmeg,
   allspice, and ground ginger

1 teaspoon baking soda
1 cup buttermilk
1-1/2 cups chopped pecans
1 cup blackberry jam

Cream butter and sugar until light and fluffy; add eggs one at a time, beating well after each addition. Sift flour, salt, and spices together. Stir baking soda into buttermilk. Add dry ingredients alternately with buttermilk to creamed mixture, beginning and ending with dry mixture.

Fold in 1 cup pecans and jam. Pour batter into three greased and floured 9-inch layer cake pans. Bake at 350°F for 30 to 35 minutes or until tests done.

Frost only between layers and on top of cake with **Buttercream Frosting**. Sprinkle remaining pecans over top.

buttercream frosting

2 cups sugar
1 cup butter
1/2 cup whipping cream

Combine all ingredients and cook without stirring until mixture reaches softball stage (234°F to 240°F). Beat until spreading consistency and quickly spread on layers.

. . . .

h e r m i t   c a k e

1 cup butter
1-1/2 cups brown sugar
3 egg yolks
2 teaspoons vanilla extract
2-1/2 cups flour
1/2 teaspoon nutmeg
1/2 teaspoon cinnamon

1-1/2 teaspoons baking powder
Juice of 1/2 fresh lemon
1 pound pitted dates, cut up
1/2 pound English walnuts, chopped
3 egg whites, stiffly beaten

Cream butter until light and fluffy; add sugar gradually, beating well. Add egg yolks one at a time, beating well after each addition. Stir in vanilla extract. Add sifted dry ingredients 1/2 cup at a time, mixing well after each addition. Pour lemon juice over dates and walnuts and stir to combine well. Dredge dates and nuts in 1/2 cup flour and fold in creamed mixture. Fold in stiffly beaten egg whites.

Pour batter into a greased and floured 10-inch tube pan. Bake at 250°F for 2 hours and 30 minutes to 3 hours. (Put a pan of water on bottom rack of oven for first 2 hours of baking).

h u m m i n g b i r d   c a k e

3 cups cake flour
2 cups sugar
1 teaspoon salt
1 teaspoon baking soda
1 teaspoon cinnamon
3 eggs, beaten

1-1/2 cups vegetable oil
1-1/2 teaspoons vanilla extract
1 (8-ounce) can crushed pineapple,
  undrained
2 cups chopped pecans, divided
2 cups chopped bananas

Combine dry ingredients; add eggs and oil, stirring until dry ingredients are moistened. Do not beat. Stir in vanilla extract, pineapple, 1 cup chopped pecans, and bananas. Spoon batter into three well-greased and floured 9-inch layer cake pans.

Bake at 350°F for 25 to 30 minutes. Cool in pans 10 minutes; remove and cool completely. Spread **Cream Cheese Frosting** between layers and on top and sides.

Sprinkle with 1 cup pecans. Cake may also be baked in a bundt or tube pan. Halve the quantities in the following frosting recipe for the bundt cake version.

cream cheese frosting

2 (8-ounce) packages cream cheese
1 cup butter
1 (16-ounce) box confectioners sugar
2 teaspoons vanilla extract

Combine cream cheese and butter, beating until light and smooth. Add sugar and vanilla extract and blend well.

. . . .

italian cream cake

1/2 cup butter
1/2 cup vegetable shortening
2 cups sugar
5 egg yolks
2 cups cake flour
1 teaspoon baking soda

1 cup buttermilk
1 teaspoon vanilla extract
1 (3.5-ounce) can flaked coconut
1 cup chopped pecans
5 egg whites, stiffly beaten

Cream butter and shortening until light and fluffy; add sugar gradually and beat well. Add egg yolks one at a time, beating well after each addition. Stir together flour and soda and add alternately with buttermilk, beating well.

Stir in vanilla extract; add coconut and pecans. Fold in egg whites.

Pour batter into 3 greased and floured 9-inch round layer cake pans. Bake at 350°F for approximately 25 minutes or until lightly browned. Cool. Frost with **Cream Cheese Frosting**.

cream cheese frosting

1 (8-ounce) package cream cheese
1 (16-ounce) box confectioners sugar
1 cup chopped pecans
1/4 stick butter
1 teaspoon vanilla extract

Mix all ingredients together until smooth. Spread between layers and over top of cake.

. . . .

jam cake

1 cup butter
1-1/2 cups sugar
4 eggs
1 teaspoon vanilla extract
3 cups cake flour
1 teaspoon baking soda
Pinch of salt

1 tablespoon cinnamon
1 tablespoon allspice
1 tablespoon nutmeg
3/4 cup buttermilk
1 cup pecans, chopped
1 cup strawberry preserves

Cream butter until fluffy; add sugar and beat until light and creamy. Add eggs one at a time, beating well after each addition. Add vanilla extract and blend well. Combine dry ingredients and sift 2 or 3 times. Add alternately with buttermilk until well blended. Stir in pecans and fold in preserves.

Pour batter into three greased and floured 9-inch round cake pans. Bake at 350°F for 25 to 30 minutes or until cakes test done. Spread **Caramel Icing** between layers and over top and sides.

caramel icing

3 cups sugar
1 cup evaporated milk
1 stick butter

1 teaspoon vanilla extract
1/4 cup sugar
1/4 cup boiling water

Combine first 4 ingredients in a saucepan and heat to melt butter. Put remaining sugar in a heavy skillet and cook on medium high until sugar has caramelized. Slowly add boiling water and stir well. Pour caramel syrup into saucepan with milk mixture. Bring to a slow boil and boil until it reaches softball stage (234°F to 240°F), stirring occasionally, approximately 8 to 10 minutes. Remove from heat and cool slightly, then beat to spreading consistency.

. . . .

lane cake

This cake appeals to the eye as well as to the palate. At least 60 years old, this family recipe has been enjoyed over and over again, especially at Christmastime.

2 sticks butter
2 cups sugar
4 eggs
3 cups sifted cake flour
3 teaspoons baking powder

1/2 teaspoon salt
1 cup evaporated milk
1 teaspoon vanilla extract
1/2 teaspoon almond extract

Cream butter; gradually add sugar, creaming until light and fluffy. Add eggs one at a time, beating well after each addition. Sift flour, baking powder, and salt together and add alternately with milk and flavorings, beating until smooth.

Pour batter into four greased and floured 9-inch round layer cake pans. Bake at 350°F for 25 to 30 minutes or until tests done. Spread **Lane Frosting** between layers and on top and sides of cake.

Recipe can also be made into two cakes by using 8-inch round layer cake pans and dividing batter equally between them. Layers will be thin.

lane frosting

2 pounds English walnuts
2 pounds Brazil nuts
1 quart pecans
2 pounds seedless raisins
Meat of 2 large coconuts

6 eggs, beaten to lemon color
2 cups sugar
2 sticks butter
2 cups evaporated milk

Coarsely grind nuts, raisins, and coconut flesh. Combine all ingredients and stir constantly over medium heat until thickened, approximately 12 minutes. Add fruits and nuts. Cool until spreading consistency, beating occasionally.

. . . .

lady baltimore cake

1 cup butter
3 cups sugar, sifted
1/4 teaspoon almond extract
1 teaspoon vanilla extract
3-1/2 cups cake flour

4 teaspoons baking powder
1/2 teaspoon salt
1 cup milk
8 egg whites
1/8 teaspoon salt

Cream butter and sugar until light and fluffy. Stir in extract. Add sifted flour, baking powder, and 1/2 teaspoon salt alternately with milk, blending thoroughly. Beat egg whites and 1/8 teaspoon salt until soft peaks form. Fold into creamed mixture. Pour into three greased and floured 9-inch layer cake pans. Bake at 350°F for 30 to 35 minutes or until tests done. **Spread White Icing** between layers and on top and sides.

white icing

2 cups sugar
1 cup water
2 egg whites

1/8 teaspoon cream of tartar
1/8 teaspoon salt
1 teaspoon vanilla extract

Boil sugar and water to soft ball stage (234°F to 240°F). Beat egg whites, cream of tartar, and salt until frothy; add syrup in a thin stream, beating constantly. Add vanilla extract. Ice cake immediately.

southern lane cake

1 cup butter
2 cups sugar
1 teaspoon vanilla extract
3-1/2 cups sifted cake flour

3 teaspoons baking powder
3/4 teaspoon salt
1 cup milk
8 egg whites

Cream butter; add sugar gradually, beating until light and fluffy. Add vanilla extract. Add sifted dry ingredients alternately with milk, beating well after each addition until smooth. Beat egg whites until stiff but not dry. Fold egg whites into batter. Pour batter into four 9-inch round layer cake pans lined on the bottom with wax paper and then greased. Bake at 350°F for approximately 25 minutes or until cakes test done. Spread with **Southern Lane Frosting**.

southern lane frosting

8 egg yolks
1-1/2 cups sugar
1/2 cup butter
1 cup evaporated milk

1 cup chopped pecans
1 cup finely chopped raisins
1 cup fresh grated coconut
1 cup finely cut candied cherries

Beat egg yolks slightly; add sugar, butter, and evaporated milk and cook over medium heat, stirring constantly until sugar has dissolved and mixture is slightly thickened. Remove from heat and add remaining ingredients. Let stand until room temperature before spreading on cake.

. . . .

layer cake no. 1

This version of the classic layer cake is light and fine textured.

2 sticks butter
2 cups sugar
5 eggs
3-1/2 cups sifted flour

3 teaspoons baking powder
1/2 teaspoon salt
1 teaspoon vanilla extract
1 cup milk

Cream butter and sugar until light and fluffy. Add eggs one at a time, beating well after each addition. Sift dry ingredients together and add alternately with milk and vanilla extract. Pour into three or four greased and lightly floured 9-inch layer cake pans. Bake at 350°F for 20 to 25 minutes or until tests done. Cool and frost with your favorite frosting.

. . . .

layer cake no. 2

For a richer tasting version of the layer cake, try this moist family favorite.

1-1/2 cups butter
2 cups sugar
4 eggs
3 cups sifted cake flour

3 teaspoons baking powder
1/2 teaspoon salt
1 cup milk
1 teaspoon vanilla extract

Cream butter and sugar until light and fluffy. Add eggs one at a time, beating well after each addition. Sift dry ingredients together and add alternately with milk and vanilla extract. Pour into three or four greased and floured 9-inch layer cake pans. Bake at 350°F for 20 to 25 minutes or until tests done. Cool and frost with your favorite frosting.

layered dessert cake

This dessert is best made one day and served the next.

Crust:
1-1/2 sticks butter
1 cup flour
1 cup chopped pecans

Melt butter; add flour and pecans. Combine well. Spread mixture over bottom of 13-1/2 x 9-inch glass baking dish. Bake at 325°F until very light brown.

Filling:
2 (8-ounce) packages cream cheese
1-1/2 cups confectioners sugar
2 boxes instant pudding (chocolate, lemon, butterscotch, or vanilla)
1 (9-ounce) carton dessert topping

Cream together cream cheese and sugar. Fold in dessert topping. Spread mixture over first layer.

Prepare 2 boxes instant pudding mix according to package directions, except use 3-1/2 cups milk. Spread over second layer.

Spread 1 large carton of dessert topping on top of final layer. Sprinkle with cut pecans and chocolate curls.

lemon cake

1 cup butter
1/2 cup vegetable shortening
2 cups granulated sugar
3 eggs
3 cups flour
1/2 teaspoon baking soda

1/2 teaspoon salt
1 cup buttermilk
2 tablespoons grated lemon zest
1/2 cup plus 1 tablespoon lemon
  juice
3 cups confectioners sugar

Beat 1/2 cup butter, shortening, and granulated sugar until light and fluffy. Add eggs one at a time, beating well after each addition. Sift flour, baking soda, and salt together and add to batter alternately with buttermilk. Stir in 1 tablespoon of lemon zest and 1 tablespoon lemon juice. Pour into a greased tube pan. Bake at 325°F for 1 hour and 15 minutes or until tests done.

Mix remaining 1/2 cup butter and confectioners sugar until creamy. Add remaining lemon zest and enough lemon juice to make pouring consistency. Pour over warm cake.

lemon cake supreme

1/3 cup butter
2/3 cup vegetable shortening
2 cups sugar
1 teaspoon vanilla extract

3-1/2 cups sifted cake flour
3 teaspoons baking powder
1 cup milk
6 egg whites, stiffly beaten

Cream butter and shortening until light; gradually add sugar, beating until light and fluffy. Add vanilla extract and then sifted dry ingredients alternately with milk. Fold in egg whites.

Pour into three greased and floured 9-inch layer cake pans. Bake at 350°F for 25 to 30 minutes or until tests done. Spread **Lemon Jelly Filling** between layers and on top and sides of cake.

lemon jelly filling

1 cup sugar
3 tablespoons cornstarch
1/2 cup hot water

Juice and grated zest of 2 lemons
6 egg yolks
1 stick butter

Combine sugar, cornstarch, hot water, juice, and zest in top of double boiler over hot water. Beat egg yolks until fluffy and add gradually to mixture in boiler. Add butter. Cook over simmering water, stirring constantly until thick enough to hold shape in spoon. Remove from heat and cool. Spread on layers of cake.

. . . .

lemon cheese cake no. 1

1 cup butter
2 cups sugar
3-1/2 cups sifted cake flour
1 teaspoon salt

2 teaspoons baking powder
1 cup milk
1 teaspoon vanilla extract
5 egg whites

Cream butter and sugar together until light and fluffy. Sift dry ingredients together 2 times; add to creamed mixture alternately with milk. Add vanilla extract. Fold in egg whites beaten stiff but not dry. Pour batter into three 9-inch layer cake pans which have been greased and floured. Bake at 350°F for 20 to 25 minutes. Spread with **Lemon Cheese Filling No. 1**.

lemon cheese filling no. 1

5 egg yolks
1 cup sugar plus 2 tablespoons
1 stick butter

Juice of 3 lemons
Grated zest of 1/2 lemon

Beat egg yolks in mixer; add sugar gradually, mixing well. Add butter and mix until creamy, then add juice and zest and cook in top of double boiler until just slightly thickened. Spread between layers and on top and sides of cake. Refrigerate unused portion.

For variation, you may wish to use **Lemon Cheese Filling** between layers and **Seven-Minute Frosting** on top and sides of cake.

. . . .

lemon cheese cake no. 2

1/2 cup vegetable shortening
1-1/2 cups sugar
3 whole eggs, slightly beaten
2-1/2 cups sifted self-rising flour
1 cup milk
1 teaspoon lemon flavoring

Cream shortening and sugar; add eggs. Add alternately to moist mixture sifted flour and milk and flavoring. Pour into three greased and floured 9-inch layer cake pans. Bake at 350°F for 25 to 30 minutes or until cakes test done. Spread with **Lemon Cheese Filling No. 2.**

lemon cheese filling no. 2

2 cups sugar
Juice of 3 lemons
Zest of 2 lemons

3 whole eggs
1/3 stick butter, melted
Pinch of salt

Combine ingredients and mix well. Cook in a double boiler (not aluminum) on medium heat, stirring often until mixture drops in flakes from spoon. Ice between layers and on top and sides. Refrigerate unused portion.

. . . .

lemon loaf

6 tablespoons butter
1 cup sugar
2 beaten eggs
1/2 cup milk
Grated zest of 1 lemon
1-1/2 cups flour

1 teaspoon baking powder
1/4 teaspoon salt
1-1/2 cups finely chopped pecans
Juice of 2 lemons combined with
   1/2 cup sugar

Cream butter and sugar until soft and fluffy. Add beaten eggs, then milk and zest. Sift dry ingredients and blend quickly into batter. Add pecans. Spoon batter into a greased loaf pan. Bake at 350°F for 1 hour and 5 minutes. Immediately after removing cake from oven, pour lemon juice and sugar mixture over warm cake.

· · · · · · · ·

lemonade cake

1/2 cup butter
3/4 cup sugar
4 eggs, separated
2 tablespoons grated lemon zest

1/4 cup lemonade concentrate
1-1/2 cups sifted cake flour
2-1/2 teaspoons baking powder
1/8 teaspoon salt

Cream butter and sugar until light and fluffy. Add egg yolks one at a time, beating well after each addition. Add zest and lemonade concentrate. Gradually add sifted dry ingredients, blending well. Add salt to egg whites and beat until stiff peaks form; gently fold into batter.

Pour mixture into a well-buttered and lightly floured square baking pan. Bake at 350°F for 30 to 35 minutes, or until tests done. Do not overbake. Cool. Dust top generously with confectioners sugar or top with lemon-flavored sweetened whipped cream.

· · · · · · · ·

swiss lemon cake

1 pound butter
3 cups sugar
6 eggs
2 ounces lemon extract

3-1/2 cups flour
1-1/2 teaspoons baking powder
1 pound golden raisins
1 pound pecans, chopped

Cream together butter and sugar until light and fluffy. Add eggs one at a time, beating well after each addition. Add lemon extract, blending well. Sift flour and baking powder together. Add to the first mixture, blending thoroughly. Add raisins and pecans. Pour into a greased tube pan. Bake at 300°F for 2 hours or until light tan and tests done.

. . . .

lemon pudding cake

1 cup sugar
5 tablespoons flour
3 egg yolks, beaten
2 tablespoons butter, melted
1 cup milk

1/4 cup freshly squeezed lemon
  juice
Grated lemon zest of 1/2 lemon
3 egg whites, stiffly beaten
Pinch of salt

Combine sugar and flour; set aside. Blend egg yolks into flour and sugar mixture. Add melted butter and blend well. Add milk, lemon juice, and zest, mixing together thoroughly. Beat egg whites and salt until stiff peaks form. Fold into first mixture. Put into pan lightly greased with margarine. Place pan in another pan of hot water. Bake 45 minutes at 350°F. (Turn out so pudding side will be up.)

. . . .

mandarin orange cake

1 box yellow cake mix
1 (11-ounce) can Mandarin oranges

4 eggs
1/4 cup vegetable oil

Combine cake mix, Mandarin oranges, eggs, and oil. Beat with electric mixer at highest speed for 2 minutes. Reduce speed to lowest speed; beat 1 minute. Pour batter into three greased and floured 9-inch layer cake pans. Bake at 350°F for 20 to 25 minutes or until tests done. Cool in pans for 5 to 10 minutes; remove layers from pans and let cool completely. Spread with **Mandarin Orange Cake Icing**.

mandarin orange cake icing

1 large (13-ounce) carton frozen whipped topping, thawed
1 large can crushed pineapple (drain and reserve juice)
1 (5-1/2 ounce) box vanilla pudding

Combine all ingredients and beat with electric mixer at medium speed for 2 minutes; let stand 5 minutes; add enough pineapple juice for spreading consistency. Spread mixture between layers and on top and sides of cake. Chill at least 2 hours before serving. Store in refrigerator.

. . . .

many flavors cake

Bake your favorite white cake. Make 6 or 7 thin layers and ice each one with a different icing.

. . . .

maple sugar cake

2 cups cake flour
2 teaspoons baking powder
1/4 teaspoon baking soda
1 teaspoon cinnamon

1/4 teaspoon nutmeg
2 eggs
1 cup soft maple sugar
1 cup sour cream

Grease two 8-inch layer cake pans. Sift flour, baking powder, baking soda, and spices 4 times. Beat eggs until light and fluffy. Add maple sugar gradually, mixing well. Add flour mixture and sour cream alternately, beginning and ending with flour mixture. Bake at 350°F for 20 minutes or until tests done. Frost with **Maple Frosting** and decorate with pecans between layers and on top of cake.

maple frosting

2/3 cup maple syrup
1/3 cup sugar
2 egg whites
2 cups pecan halves

Stir together maple syrup and sugar. Cook slowly to soft ball stage (234°F to 240°F). Beat egg whites until soft peaks form. Pour cooked syrup into egg whites in a thin, steady stream, beating constantly with electric mixer. Keep beating until frosting starts to cool. Put pecan halves on 1 layer and cover it with frosting; put frosting on top layer and decorate with pecans.

. . . .

mississippi mud cake no. 1

1-1/2 sticks butter (3/4 cup)
1-1/2 cups sugar
4 eggs
1 teaspoon vanilla extract
1-3/4 cups cake flour
1 teaspoon baking powder

1/2 teaspoon salt
1/2 cup cocoa
1/2 cup heavy cream
1/2 cup cold coffee
4 (1.2 ounce) milk chocolate bars

Grease and flour an 11-3/4 x 7-1/2 x 1-3/4-inch baking pan. Preheat oven to 350°F. Cream butter and sugar until light and fluffy. Add eggs one at a time, beating well after each addition. Add vanilla extract and blend well. Add sifted dry ingredients alternately with cream and coffee. Pour into prepared pan. Bake for 350°F for 40 minutes or until tests done.

Break chocolate into pieces and place on hot cake and let stand 1 minute, then spread softened chocolate to frost cake. Cool before serving.

mississippi mud cake no. 2

4 eggs
1-3/4 cups sugar
1 cup vegetable oil
1/3 cup cocoa

1-1/2 cups self-rising flour
3 teaspoons vanilla extract
2 cups chopped pecans
2 cups miniature marshmallows

Grease and flour an 11-3/4 x 7-1/2 x 1-3/4-inch baking pan. Preheat oven to 300°F. Beat eggs until fluffy; add sugar gradually, blending well. Add oil. Sift cocoa and flour together and add to batter alternately with vanilla extract. Blend in pecans. Pour into prepared pan. Bake at 300°F for 40 to 45 minutes. Cover with miniature marshmallows and the following **Mississippi Mud Cake Glaze** while cake is still warm:

mississippi mud cake glaze

1-1/2 sticks butter
1 teaspoon vanilla extract
1 (16-ounce) box confectioners
  sugar

1/3 cup cocoa
1/2 cup whipping cream
1-1/2 cups chopped pecans

Combine well and spread over cake while it is still warm. Cool cake before serving.

. . . .

melt-in-your-mouth cake

1-1/2 cups butter, softened
3-1/2 cups confectioners sugar
6 eggs

3-1/2 cups sifted cake flour
1 tablespoon vanilla extract

Cream butter until smooth. Add sugar gradually and beat until light and fluffy. Add eggs one at a time, beating well after each addition. Add cake flour and vanilla extract and beat well. Spoon batter into a greased 10-inch tube pan. Bake at 325°F for 45 minutes or until tests done.

. . . .

orange florida-style cake

Cake:
1 cup butter
1-1/2 cups sugar
4 eggs
2-1/2 cups cake flour
2 teaspoons baking powder

1/2 teaspoon salt
1/4 cup freshly squeezed orange
  juice
1 tablespoons grated orange zest

Filling:
3 tablespoons flour
2 tablespoons cornstarch
1/2 cup sugar
1 cup orange juice
1 teaspoon grated orange zest

1 teaspoon unflavored gelatin
1 tablespoon water
2 egg yolks, lightly beaten
1/4 cup butter
1/2 cup heavy cream, whipped

Frosting:
2 egg whites
1-3/4 cups sugar
1 tablespoon light corn syrup
5 tablespoons orange juice

To prepare cake: Cream butter with sugar; add eggs one at a time. Add sifted flour, baking powder, and salt alternately with juice and zest. Pour mixture into two greased and floured 9-inch layer cake pans. Bake at 325°F for approximately 30 minutes or until tests done.

To prepare filling: Combine flour, cornstarch, and sugar in small pan. Add orange juice and orange zest and mix well. Soak gelatin in water. Bring orange juice mixture to a boil, stirring constantly. Cook 2 minutes. Spoon a little hot mixture into egg yolks and mix. Add remaining orange mixture. Cook 1/2 minute longer. Add soaked gelatin and butter. Stir to dissolve. Cool and chill, stirring occasionally. Fold in whipped cream just before spreading on cake layers.

To prepare frosting: Place all ingredients in top of double boiler over rapidly boiling water. Beat with electric mixer for approximately 7 minutes or until soft, stiff peaks form.

. . . .

orange cake

1 navel orange
1/2 cup ground pecans
1/2 cup pitted dates
1/2 cup plumped raisins
1/2 cup butter
1-1/2 cups sugar

3 eggs
2 cups cake flour
1 teaspoon baking soda
1 teaspoon salt
1/2 cup buttermilk

Grind pecans, dates, and raisins. Stir orange juice and zest into ground mixture; set aside.

Cream butter and sugar together until light and fluffy. Add eggs one at a time, beating well after each addition. Sift flour, baking soda, and salt together and add alternately with buttermilk. Beat in ground mixture very well. Grease and flour a tube pan or bundt pan. Bake at 325°F for 1 hour and 15 minutes or until tests done. Cool completely, then spread with **Orange Buttercream Frosting**.

orange buttercream frosting

1-1/2 cups butter, softened
4-1/2 cups confectioners sugar
2 tablespoons orange juice
1 tablespoon grated orange zest

Combine butter and sugar, creaming until well blended. Add orange juice and beat until smooth. Stir in orange zest. Spread on cake immediately.

. . . .

old fashioned plain cake

1 stick margarine
1/2 cup shortening
2 cups sugar
5 large eggs
2 cups cake flour

2 tablespoons fresh orange juice or
diluted orange juice concentrate
2 teaspoons extract (1 teaspoon
lemon and 1 teaspoon vanilla or
almond)

Beat margarine, shortening, and sugar until light and creamy. Add eggs one at a time, beating well after each addition. Sift flour 3 times (1 time before measuring, 2 after). Add flour, then juice and extracts alternately, blending well after each addition. Pour batter into a greased and floured bundt pan. Bake at 325°F for 1 hour and 5 minutes or until tests done. Cool in pan for 10 minutes, then turn out onto wire rack. Drizzle with **Orange Juice Glaze**, if desired.

orange sour cream cake

1 cup butter
1-1/2 cups sugar
3 eggs, separated
2 cups flour
1 teaspoon baking powder
1 teaspoon baking soda

1 cup sour cream
Grated zest of 1 orange
1/2 cup chopped pecans
1/2 cup fresh orange juice
2 tablespoons slivered almonds,
blanched

Cream together butter and 1 cup sugar until light and fluffy. Beat in egg yolks. Sift flour, baking powder, and baking soda and add alternately with sour cream. Stir in orange zest and nuts. Beat egg whites and fold into batter. Bake in greased 9-inch tube pan at 325°F for approximately 50 minutes.

Combine orange juice and remaining sugar and mix well. Spoon over hot cake. Decorate with almonds. Cool cake before removing from pan.

peach crumb cake

1-1/2 cups sifted cake flour
1/2 cup sugar
Pinch of salt
1/2 cup butter, softened
4 cups sliced, peeled fresh peaches

1/2 cup sugar
3 tablespoons quick-cooking
   tapioca
1 tablespoon lemon juice

Combine flour, 1/2 cup sugar, and salt. Cut in butter until mixture resembles coarse crumbs. Measure 3/4 cup into medium mixing bowl; set aside. Press remaining flour mixture into bottom and approximately 3/4 inch up sides of a 9-inch springform pan. Bake crust at 425°F for 5 to 10 minutes or until lightly browned. Cool.

Mix peaches, 1/2 cup sugar, tapioca, and lemon juice. Arrange in bottom of cooled crust. Bake at 425°F for 20 minutes; then sprinkle with reserved flour mixture. Continue baking 20 to 25 minutes longer or until top is golden brown. Serve warm or cold with sweetened whipped cream, if desired.

May also be baked in a 9-inch flan ring, but do not pre-bake crust.

orange buttermilk cake

1 cup butter
2 cups sugar
4 eggs
1 teaspoon baking soda
1-1/3 cups buttermilk

4 cups cake flour
2 tablespoons grated orange zest
1 cup dates, chopped
1 cups pecans, chopped

Cream butter and sugar. Beat in eggs one at a time, beating well after each addition. Dissolve soda in buttermilk. Add sifted flour alternately with buttermilk, beating well after each addition until smooth. Dredge orange zest, dates, and nuts in flour and add to batter. Bake in tube pan at 325°F for approximately 1 hour and 30 minutes. When cake is done, pour **Sauce** over cake and cool in pan. Serve with sweetened whipped cream, if desired.

sauce for orange buttermilk cake

2 cups sugar
1 cup orange juice, freshly squeezed
2 tablespoons orange zest

Beat with electric mixer until sugar is dissolved. Do not heat.

. . . .

peach sour cream cake

1 (18-1/2 ounce) box butter-flavor
  cake mix
1-1/2 cups sugar
4 tablespoons cornstarch
4 cups chopped fresh peaches
1/2 cup water

2 cups whipping cream
2 to 3 tablespoons confectioners
  sugar
1 cup sour cream
Fresh sliced peaches (optional)

Prepare cake according to package directions, using two 8-inch layer cake pans. Cool, then split each layer.

Combine sugar and cornstarch in a saucepan. Add peaches and water; cook over medium heat, stirring constantly, until smooth and thickened. Cool mixture completely.

Combine whipping cream and confectioners sugar in a medium mixing bowl; beat until stiff peaks form.

Spoon 1/3 of the peach filling over split layer of cake; spread 1/3 sour cream over filling. Repeat procedure with remaining cake layers, peach filling, and sour cream, ending with remaining cake layer. Frost with sweetened whipped cream and garnish with fresh peach slices.

. . . .

peach marshmallow cake

1/2 cup butter
1 cup granulated sugar
1 egg
2 cups cake flour
1/4 teaspoon salt
2 teaspoons baking powder

3/4 cup milk
6 canned peach halves
1/4 cup light brown sugar
1 teaspoon cinnamon
1 tablespoon butter
6 small marshmallows

Cream 1/2 cup butter with 1 cup granulated sugar. Add egg and mix well. Sift flour, salt, and baking powder together and add alternately with milk until well blended.

Pour into a greased 10 x 7-inch pan. Arrange peach halves, cut side up. Sprinkle brown sugar and cinnamon over peaches. Dot with butter. Bake at 350°F for 30 minutes. Place marshmallow in each peach halve and return to oven. Brown lightly.

. . . .

orange marmalade cake

3/4 cup butter, softened
1 cup sugar
3 eggs
1 cup orange marmalade
4-1/4 cups cake flour
1-1/2 teaspoons baking soda

1 teaspoon salt
1/2 cup evaporated milk
1/2 cup fresh orange juice
1 teaspoon vanilla extract
1 tablespoon grated orange zest
1 cup chopped pecans

Cream butter and sugar thoroughly. Add eggs one at a time, beating well after each addition. Add marmalade, mixing well. Sift flour, baking soda, and salt together. Add this alternately with milk and orange juice. Stir in vanilla extract, orange zest, and pecans well.

Pour batter into a greased and floured 10-inch tube pan. Bake at 350°F for 1 hour and 5 minutes or until tests done. Cool in pan for 10 minutes; remove and cool completely. Frost cake with **Orange Whipped Cream**.

orange whipped cream

1 cup whipping cream
2 tablespoons sugar
1 tablespoon grated orange zest

Beat whipping cream until foamy; gradually add sugar, beating until soft peaks form. Stir in zest.

. . . .

orange pecan cake

1/2 cup butter, softened
1/4 cup shortening
1-1/2 cups sugar
3 eggs
3 cups cake flour
1-1/2 teaspoons baking soda

3/4 teaspoon salt
1-1/2 cups buttermilk
1-1/2 teaspoons vanilla extract
1 cup chopped golden raisins
1 cup finely chopped pecans
1 tablespoon grated orange zest

Cream together butter, shortening, and sugar. Add eggs one at a time, beating well after each addition. Add sifted flour, baking soda, and salt alternately with buttermilk and vanilla extract; mix just until blended and beat with electric mixer at high speed for 3 minutes.

Stir raisins, pecans, and zest into batter and pour into three greased and floured layer cake pans. Bake at 350°F for 30 to 35 minutes or until tests done. Cool 5 to 10 minutes in pans; remove and cool completely.

Spread **Orange Buttercream Frosting** between layers and on top and sides of cake.

orange buttercream frosting

1-1/2 cups butter, softened
4-1/2 cups confectioners sugar
1 tablespoon orange juice
1 tablespoon grated orange zest

Combine butter and sugar, creaming until light and fluffy. Add orange juice; beat until spreading consistency. Stir in orange zest.

. . . .

orange shortcake

Pastry:
3 cups all-purpose flour
1 tablespoon sugar
2 teaspoons salt

1 cup vegetable oil
1/4 cup milk

Sauce:
12 to 16 medium oranges
3/4 cup sugar
1/3 cup butter
1 tablespoon cornstarch

3/4 cup water
1-1/2 teaspoons lemon juice
1/2 teaspoon grated orange zest

To prepare pastry: Combine dry ingredients; add oil and milk, stirring until mixture forms a ball. Roll dough out on a lightly floured surface to 1/8-inch thickness. Cut into rounds with a 2-1/2-inch biscuit cutter. Using a metal spatula, lift rounds and place on a lightly greased baking sheet. Bake at 350°F for 18 to 20 minutes or until lightly browned. (Pastry will be very fragile.) Cool on wire racks.

To prepare sauce: Peel and section enough oranges to make 5 cups of orange sections; drain, reserving 3/4 cup juice. Set aside 1 cup of sections for topping.

Combine sugar, butter, orange juice, cornstarch, water, lemon juice, and zest in a medium saucepan. Cook over low heat, stirring constantly, until slightly thickened and bubbling. Remove from heat; stir in 4 cups orange sections.

Place 1 pastry round on each serving dish; cover each with 1/3 cup orange sauce. Top with remaining pastry rounds. Spoon remaining orange sauce over each. Garnish with a dollop of sweetened whipped cream and an orange section.

peanut graham cake

1 cup dark brown sugar
1/2 cup granulated sugar
2/3 cup butter
1/3 cup creamy peanut butter
3 eggs
2 cups cake flour
1 teaspoon baking powder

1/2 teaspoon cinnamon
1 teaspoon baking soda
1 cup graham cracker crumbs
1 cup orange juice
1 cup chopped roasted cocktail
  peanuts

Cream together sugars, butter, and peanut butter until light and fluffy. Add eggs one at a time, beating well after each addition. Add sifted dry ingredients to batter alternately with orange juice, blending well. Stir in peanuts. Pour into a greased and floured 10-inch tube pan or 12-cup bundt pan. Bake at 350°F for 50 minutes or until tests done.

Cool in pan for approximately 15 minutes. Remove to wire rack; glaze with **Peanut Glaze**.

peanut glaze

2 tablespoons dark brown sugar
2 tablespoons milk
1 tablespoon butter
2 teaspoons creamy peanut butter

1 cup confectioners sugar
1/2 teaspoon vanilla extract
1/4 cup chopped roasted cocktail
  peanuts

In saucepan, combine brown sugar, milk, butter, and peanut butter; heat until melted. Stir in remaining ingredients and beat until smooth.

peanut cake

1-1/2 cups sifted cake flour
1 teaspoon baking soda
1/3 cup shortening
1 cup sugar
1 egg
1 teaspoon vanilla extract

1 cup sour cream
1 (6-1/2-ounce) can salted Spanish
  peanuts, chopped
1 (6-ounce) package sweet milk
  chocolate chips

Sift flour and baking soda together. Cream together shortening and sugar until light and fluffy. Add egg, beat well. Add vanilla extract. Add dry ingredients alternately with sour cream. Stir in peanuts. Pour into a greased 9-inch square pan. Bake at 350°F for 30 minutes. Sprinkle chocolate chips over top and place cake in oven until they begin to melt. Remove and spread chocolate over top. Cool in pan on wire rack.

peanut butter cake

3/4 cup butter
3/4 cup creamy peanut butter
2 cups firmly packed brown sugar
3 eggs
1 teaspoon vanilla extract

2-1/2 cups cake flour
1 tablespoon baking powder
1/2 teaspoon salt
1 cup milk
1/2 cup chopped peanuts

Cream butter and peanut butter well. Add sugar and cream until light and fluffy. Add eggs one at a time, beating well after each addition. Add vanilla extract. Sift flour, baking powder, and salt together; add to creamed mixture alternately with milk, beating well. Spoon into a greased 13 x 9 x 2-inch baking pan. Bake at 350°F for 45 to 50 minutes or until tests done. When cool, spread with **Chocolate Frosting** and sprinkle with chopped peanuts.

chocolate frosting

1 (6-ounce) package semisweet chocolate morsels
1/3 cup evaporated milk
1-1/2 cups confectioners sugar

Combine chocolate morsels and milk in a medium saucepan and place over low heat, stirring until melted. Stir in sugar and beat until smooth.

. . . .

pear cake

2 cups sugar
3 eggs, well beaten
1-1/2 cups vegetable oil
3 cups cake flour
1 teaspoon baking soda

1 teaspoon salt
1 teaspoon vanilla extract
2 teaspoons cinnamon
3 cups thinly sliced pears

Combine sugar, eggs, and oil; beat well. Combine flour, baking soda, and salt; add to sugar mixture 1 cup at a time, mixing well after each addition. Stir in vanilla extract, cinnamon, and pears. Spoon batter into a well-greased 10-inch bundt pan. Bake at 350°F for 1 hour. Allow to cool and top with **Confectioners Sugar Glaze**.

confectioners sugar glaze

1-1/4 cups sifted confectioners sugar
2 to 4 tablespoons milk

Blend these ingredients well and pour over cooled cake.

. . . .

fondant for petit fours

1-1/4 cups water
4 cups sugar
1/2 cup white corn syrup

Boil water and sugar together for approximately 5 minutes. When syrup reaches soft ball stage (234°F to 240°F), add corn syrup and bring to boiling point again. Remove and pour onto a buttered platter. Cool until lukewarm, then using a spatula pull sides into middle repeatedly until mixture turns white and thick. Let stand 5 minutes. Then knead with buttered hands until creamy enough to form a firm ball. Butter hands heavily to soften. Store fondant in a tightly covered container for at least 2 days before using. To prepare fondant for frosting cakes, warm 1 or 2 cups slowly over hot, but not boiling, water. Tint with a few drops of food coloring or flavoring, if desired. To thin fondant, add a few drops of hot water.

pecan cake

3 eggs
1 cup sugar
1 cup chopped pecans
1 teaspoon vanilla extract

Pinch of salt
2-1/2 cups vanilla wafers, rolled
   into crumbs
1 teaspoon baking powder

Beat eggs until thick; add sugar gradually; add nuts, vanilla extract, and salt. Add crumbs and baking powder. Grease two 8-inch layer cake pans and line with waxed paper, grease again. Pour batter into pan. Bake at 275°F for 25 minutes. Cool. Spread whipped cream mixed with a few chopped pecans and sweetened with brown sugar between layers. Top with whipped cream and whole pecans.

mississippi pecan cake

1/2 cup butter	3 cups flour
2 cups sugar	3 teaspoons baking powder
1 egg	3/4 teaspoon salt
3 egg yolks	1 cup milk
1 teaspoon vanilla extract	Pecan Mixture

Cream butter and sugar until light and fluffy; add egg and yolks one at a time, beating well after each addition. Add vanilla extract. Sift dry ingredients together and add alternately with milk, blending well. Grease a 10-inch tube pan and line bottom only with waxed paper. Pour 1/2 batter into pan. Drop **Pecan Mixture** by spoonful onto batter, then top with remaining batter. Bake at 325°F for 1 hour and 25 minutes or until tests done. Cool in pan on wire rack.

pecan mixture

3 egg whites	2 tablespoons all-purpose flour
1/4 teaspoon salt	1 teaspoon baking powder
1/4 cup water	1 pound (4 cups) ground pecans.
1/2 cup sugar	

Combine egg whites, salt, and water. Beat at high speed until stiff but not dry. Stir together sugar, flour, and baking powder. Gradually beat into egg whites until stiff. Fold in ground pecans.

pecan spice cake

1 cup vegetable shortening
2 cups sugar
4 beaten eggs
3 cups sifted flour
1 teaspoon baking powder

1 teaspoon baking soda
1-1/2 teaspoons cinnamon
1/2 teaspoon ground cloves
1 cup buttermilk
2 cups chopped pecans

Cream shortening and sugar until light and fluffy. Add beaten eggs and blend well. Sift dry ingredients together 3 times and add alternately with buttermilk, blending well after each addition. Stir in pecans. Pour into a greased tube pan. Bake at 350°F for 1 hour.

. . . .

pecan supreme loaf

1 (8-ounce) package cream cheese, softened
1 cup butter
1-1/4 cups sugar
4 eggs
1 teaspoon grated orange zest

1/2 teaspoon orange extract
2-1/2 cups cake flour
2 teaspoons baking powder
1/2 teaspoon salt
3/4 cup finely chopped pecans

Cream together cream cheese, butter, and sugar, beating until very light and fluffy. Add eggs one at a time, beating well after each addition. Add orange zest and extract and blend well. Add sifted dry ingredients and blend well. Stir in pecans just until blended. Pour into a greased and floured 9 x 5-inch loaf pan. Bake at 325°F for 1 hour and 10 minutes.

. . . .

perfect cake

1 cup butter
2 cups sugar
5 eggs
1 teaspoon vanilla extract

3-1/2 cups cake flour
2-1/2 teaspoons baking powder
1/4 teaspoon salt
1 cup milk

Cream butter and sugar until light and fluffy. Add eggs one at a time, beating well after each addition. Blend in vanilla extract. Sift flour, baking powder, and salt together, add alternately with milk, blending thoroughly. Pour batter into three or four 9-inch layer cake pans. Bake at 350°F for 20 to 25 minutes or until tests done.

Frost between layers and on top and sides with **Perfect Cake Icing. Seven-Minute Frosting** may be used instead of the cooked frosting; however, cooked frosting holds its shape longer.

perfect cake icing

2 cups sugar
1 cup water
1/4 cup white corn syrup
3 egg whites, stiffly beaten
1 teaspoon vanilla extract
1 fresh coconut, grated

1 small can pineapple, crushed, and
  well drained
1 cup chopped pecans
1 small bottle maraschino cherries,
  chopped in small pieces

Boil sugar, water, and syrup together until it spins a thread from the spoon. Beating constantly, pour in a very thin stream slowly over stiffly beaten egg whites. Beat until stiff enough to hold its shape. Blend in vanilla extract and add coconut, pineapple, pecans, and cherries. Spread immediately on cake.

. . . .

petit fours

4 eggs
1/2 cup granulated sugar
1 teaspoon grated lemon zest

1 cup flour
1/2 stick butter, melted

Combine eggs, sugar, and lemon zest. With electric mixer, beat mixture in pan placed over boiling water until sugar has dissolved. Remove from heat and beat until cool. Slowly fold in flour and then melted butter poured into the batter in a thin stream. Pour batter into a buttered and lightly floured 8-inch square baking pan. Bake at 350°F for approximately 25 minutes or until tests done. Cut cooled cake into small diamonds or squares. With cakes pierced onto a fork, dip into **Fondant. Buttercream Icing** or a boiled icing may be used instead of the **Fondant. Pound Cake** may be used instead of the recipe above.

. . . .

pineapple cream cheese cake

3-1/2 cups cake flour
2 cups sugar
1 teaspoon baking soda
1 teaspoon salt
1 teaspoon ground cloves
3 eggs, beaten

1-1/4 cups vegetable oil
1 teaspoon almond extract
1 (8-ounce) can crushed pineapple, undrained
1 cup chopped toasted almonds
2 cups mashed banana

Combine first 5 ingredients in a large mixing bowl; add eggs and oil, stirring until dry ingredients are moistened. Do not beat. Stir in almond extract, pineapple, almonds, and banana.

Spoon batter into a greased and floured 10-inch tube pan. Bake at 300°F for 1 hour and 15 minutes. Cool in pan 10 minutes; remove cake from pan and cool completely. Frost with **Cream Cheese Frosting**.

cream cheese frosting

1/2 cup butter, softened
1 (8-ounce) package cream cheese, softened
1 (16-ounce) box confectioners sugar

1 tablespoon instant tea
1/8 teaspoon salt

Cream butter and cream cheese; gradually add sugar, tea, and salt, beating until very light and fluffy.

· · · · · · · · · ·

pineapple cake

1/4 cup butter
20 graham crackers, rolled fine
2 tablespoons sugar
3 eggs, separated
1(15-ounce) can sweetened condensed milk

Juice and grated zest of 1 lemon
1-1/2 cups crushed pineapple, drained

Melt butter over low heat. Crush graham crackers into fine crumbs. Add sugar and melted butter to crumbs and mix well. Pat 1/2 the mixture in bottom of 8-inch springform pan.

Beat egg yolks until light yellow in color. Add condensed milk, lemon juice, zest and pineapple, blending well. Beat egg whites until they hold a peak. Carefully fold them into pineapple and condensed milk mixture. Spoon gently into crumb-lined pan. Sprinkle remaining crumbs on top.

Bake at 325°F for 1 hour. Cool. Serve with sweetened whipped cream.

· · · · · · · · · ·

pineapple layer cake

1 cup butter, softened	3 1/2 cups cake flour
2 cups granulated sugar	3 teaspoons baking powder
5 large eggs	1/8 teaspoon salt
1 tablespoon pineapple juice	1 cup whole milk

In a large mixing bowl, cream butter and sugar together until light and fluffy. Add eggs, one at a time, beating well after each addition. Stir in pineapple juice. Sift flour, baking powder, and salt together. Add alternately with milk, beginning and ending with flour mixture. Pour into three or four greased and floured 9-inch layer cake pans. Bake at 350°F for 25 to 30 minutes or until cakes test done. Cool cakes on wire racks for approximately 5 minutes before removing from pans. Cool completely and spread **Pineapple Filling** between layers and on top and sides of cake.

pineapple filling and frosting

3/4 cup butter, melted
1 1/2 cups granulated sugar
6 large egg yolks, lightly beaten
4 tablespoons sifted all-purpose flour
1 (20-ounce) can crushed pineapple, well drained

In top of a double boiler over boiling water, combine melted butter and sugar. Stir until mixture is smooth and blended well. Gradually stir in beaten egg yolks, a small amount at a time. Slowly add flour and then pineapple. Cook and stir in top of double boiler until mixture is thickened. Cool and spread on cooled layers and over top and sides of cake.

. . . .

pineapple carrot cake

1-1/2 cups vegetable oil
2 cups sugar
3 eggs
3 cups cake flour
1 teaspoon baking powder

1/2 teaspoon salt
1 teaspoon cinnamon
1 (8-ounce) can crushed pineapple
2 cups finely shredded carrots
Confectioners sugar

Beat together oil and sugar until well blended. Add eggs one at a time, beating well after each addition. Sift dry ingredients and blend into batter well. Add pineapple and carrots and pour into a greased and floured 13 x 9 x 2-inch pan. Bake at 350°F for approximately 45 minutes. Cool in pan. Sprinkle with confectioners sugar and cut into squares.

. . . .

pineapple loaf

3 sticks butter
3 cups confectioners sugar
6 eggs
1 teaspoon vanilla extract

1 teaspoon lemon juice
2 cups cake flour
1 (20-ounce) can crushed pineapple,
   well drained

Cream butter and sugar until light and fluffy. Add eggs one at a time, beating well after each addition. Add vanilla extract and lemon juice. Stir in flour, mix well. Add drained pineapple. Spoon into a greased and floured 10-inch tube pan. Bake at 350°F for 1 hours and 30 minutes. No frosting needed.

. . . .

pineapple cream roll

3/4 cup sifted cake flour
3/4 teaspoon baking powder
1/4 teaspoon salt
4 eggs

3/4 cup sugar
1 teaspoon vanilla extract
Confectioners sugar

Sift flour, baking powder, and salt. Beat eggs until light and lemon-colored, approximately 10 minutes. Gradually add sugar, beating well after each addition. Add vanilla extract. Fold in dry ingredients. Spread batter in wax paper-lined 15-1/2 x 10-1/2 x 1-inch jellyroll pan. Bake at 375°F for 13 minutes.

Turn out onto dish towel dusted with confectioners sugar. Roll up starting at long side. Cool for 10 minutes. Unroll cake and spread with **Pineapple Cream Filling** to within 1/2 inch of edges. Start rolling up cake from long end. Cool thoroughly. Refrigerate until serving time.

pineapple cream filling

1/2 cup sugar
2 tablespoons cornstarch
2 tablespoons flour
1/4 teaspoon salt
2 cups milk

2 egg yolks
1 (8-1/2-ounce) can crushed
   pineapple, drained
8 maraschino cherries, quartered
1 teaspoon vanilla extract

Combine sugar, cornstarch, flour, and salt in small saucepan. Stir in milk. Cook, stirring constantly, until mixture thickens. Mix some of the hot mixture with egg yolks. Then stir egg mixture into hot mixture. Cook for 1 minute. Add pineapple, maraschino cherries, and vanilla extract. Cool.

plum cake

2 cups self-rising flour	3 eggs
2 cups sugar	1 cup chopped dates
1 teaspoon cinnamon	1 cup chopped pecans
3/4 cup vegetable oil	2 small jars of plum baby food

Mix all ingredients together with electric mixer until well blended. Pour into greased and floured bundt pan. Bake at 350°F for 1 hour or until tests done. Spread with **Confectioners Sugar Icing**.

confectioners sugar icing

1 cup confectioners sugar
Juice of 1 lemon

Add enough lemon juice to confectioners sugar for a thin frosting. Spread over cake while still warm. Prick cake with a fork to allow icing to seep into cake.

pineapple upside-down cake

3 tablespoons butter, melted	2 eggs
1 cup firmly packed brown sugar	1-1/2 cups all-purpose flour
1 (15-1/2-ounce) can sliced pineapple, drained	2 teaspoons baking powder
1/2 cup shortening	1/2 teaspoon salt
1 cup sugar	2/3 cup milk
	1 teaspoon vanilla extract

Melt butter in a 10-inch cast iron skillet. Spread brown sugar evenly over butter. Arrange pineapple on sugar.

Cream shortening and sugar until light and fluffy. Add eggs one at a time, mixing well after each addition.

Stir in remaining ingredients; beat 2 minutes or until batter is smooth and fluffy.

Spoon batter evenly over pineapple slices. Bake at 350°F for 50 to 55 minutes or until tests done. Cool 5 minutes, and invert cake onto serving plate.

. . . .

poppy seed cake

3/4 cup poppy seeds	2 tablespoons baking powder
1/2 cup butter	3/4 cup milk
1-1/2 cups sugar	4 egg whites
2 cups flour	1 teaspoon vanilla extract

Soak seeds in milk 5 to 6 hours. Cream butter and sugar until light and fluffy. Add seeds and blend well. Add sifted flour and baking powder alternately with milk; then fold in stiffly beaten egg whites and vanilla extract. Pour into three greased and floured 9-inch layer cake pans. Bake at 350°F for 30 minutes or until tests done. Spread **Pecan Filling** between layers and **Cocoa Frosting** on top and sides of cake.

pecan filling

3 tablespoons cornstarch
1 cup sugar
1/4 teaspoon salt
4 egg yolks
2 cups milk
1 cup chopped pecans

Mix cornstarch, sugar, and salt. Beat egg yolks, add milk and combine with sugar mixture. Cook in double boiler, stirring constantly, until thick. Remove from heat; add pecans and cool. Spread between layers.

cocoa frosting

1/2 cup butter
3 cups confectioners sugar
4 tablespoons cocoa

2 teaspoons vanilla extract
Brewed coffee

Cream butter and sugar; add cocoa and vanilla extract. Moisten with enough cold strong coffee to spread over top and sides of cake.

. . . .

prune cake

1-1/2 cups dried prunes
1 teaspoon grated lemon zest
2 cups sifted all-purpose flour
1 teaspoon baking powder
1 teaspoon baking soda
1/2 teaspoon salt
1 cup butter, softened
1 cup sugar

1/2 cup light brown sugar
3 eggs
1 teaspoon vanilla extract
1 cup sour cream
1/2 cup light brown sugar
1 tablespoon cinnamon
1/2 cup chopped pecans

Prepare dried prunes as directed on package. Drain, pit, and dice and sprinkle with lemon zest; set aside. Sift flour, baking powder, baking soda, and salt together. Take out 1/4 cup of mixture and toss with prunes.

Cream butter and sugars, beating until light and fluffy. Add eggs one at a time, beating well after each addition. Stir in vanilla extract. Add sifted dry ingredients alternately with sour cream. Fold in prunes.

Combine 1/2 cup brown sugar with cinnamon and nuts.

Pour 1/3 of the batter into greased and floured 9-inch bundt or tube pan. Sprinkle over 1/2 of the cinnamon and nut mixture, 1/3 of the batter, remaining cinnamon and nut mixture; top with remaining batter.

Bake in 350°F for approximately 55 minutes or until tests done. Cool in pan for 10 minutes; remove. Pour over cake a glaze made of juice and grated zest of 1 lemon and 1 cup of confectioners sugar.

. . . .

praline ice cream cake

2 cups cake flour	1/2 cup butter
1 cup sugar	1 pint vanilla ice cream, softened
1 cup graham cracker crumbs	2 eggs, beaten
1 tablespoon baking powder	Brown Sugar Topping
1/2 teaspoon salt	1/2 cup chopped pecans

Combine first 5 ingredients in medium mixing bowl; set aside.

Melt butter over low heat and remove. Add ice cream, flour mixture, and eggs; stir until batter is smooth.

Pour batter into a lightly greased 13 x 9 x 2-inch baking pan; spoon 1/3 cup **Brown Sugar Topping** over batter. Bake at 350°F for 30 minutes or until tests done.

Stir pecans into remaining 2/3 cup topping; spread immdediately over hot cake. Cool on wire rack.

brown sugar topping

1 cup firmly packed brown sugar	2 teaspoons cornstarch
1/2 cup sour cream	1/2 teaspoon vanilla extract
2 tablespoons butter	

Combine all ingredients except vanilla extract in a small saucepan; cook over medium heat until thickened and bubbly, stirring constantly. Remove from heat and stir in vanilla extract.

. . . .

pumpkin cake

2 cups sugar
1 (16-ounce) can pumpkin
   (or 2 cups cooked, mashed fresh
   pumpkin)
1 cup vegetable oil
4 eggs, beaten
1 teaspoon salt

2 cups all-purpose flour
2 teaspoons baking soda
2 teaspoons baking powder
2 teaspoons cinnamon
1/2 cup flaked coconut
1/2 cup chopped pecans

Combine sugar, pumpkin, oil, and eggs; beat with electric mixer at medium speed for 1 minute. Combine next 5 ingredients; add to pumpkin mixture. Beat 1 minute at medium speed. Stir in coconut and pecans. Pour batter into three greased and floured 9-inch layer cake pans. Bake at 350°F for 25 minutes or until tests done. Cool in pans 10 minutes; remove and cool completely. Spread **Cream Cheese Frosting** between layers and on top of cake.

cream cheese frosting

1/2 cup butter, softened
1 (8-ounce) package cream cheese,
   softened
1 (16-ounce) box confectioners
   sugar

2 teaspoons vanilla extract
1/2 cup chopped pecans
1/2 cup flaked coconut

Combine butter and cream cheese; beat until light and fluffy. Add sugar and vanilla extract, mixing well. Stir in pecans and coconut.

. . . .

pumpkin layer cake

1 cup vegetable oil	1/4 teaspoon salt
2 cups granulated sugar	2 teaspoons cinnamon
4 large eggs	1 (16-ounce) can pumpkin
2 1/2 cups cake flour	(or 2 cups cooked, mashed fresh
2 teaspoons baking soda	pumpkin)
1 teaspoon baking powder	

In a large mixing bowl, combine oil and sugar. Beat until mixed thoroughly. Add eggs one at a time, beating well after each addition. Sift flour, baking soda, baking powder, salt, and cinnamon together. Slowly add to oil and sugar mixture, beating until well blended. Stir in pumpkin. Pour into two or three greased and floured 9-inch layer cake pans. Bake at 350°F for approximately 30 minutes or until cakes test done. Cool in pans on a wire rack for approximately 5 minutes; remove from pan and cool completely. Frost with **Cream Cheese Frosting** between and on top and sides of cake.

cream cheese frosting

1/2 cup butter, softened
1 (8-ounce) carton cream cheese, softened
1 (16-ounce) box confectioners sugar, sifted
2 teaspoons vanilla extract

In a large mixing bowl, cream butter and cream cheese until smooth. Gradually add confectioners sugar, then add flavoring. Beat until well blended. Spread on cooled cakes.

pumpkin bread

2 cups sugar
4 eggs
1 teaspoon nutmeg
1 teaspoon cinnamon
1-1/2 teaspoons salt

1 cup vegetable oil
1 cup canned pumpkin
2/3 cup water
2 teaspoons baking soda
3 cups sifted flour

Blend together sugar, eggs, spices, salt, and oil. Stir in pumpkin, water, baking soda, and flour. Blend well. Fill three greased and floured 1-pound coffee cans 1/2 full of batter. Bake at 350°F for 50 to 55 minutes.

. . . .

red velvet cake no. 1

2-1/2 cups sifted flour
1 teaspoon baking soda
1 teaspoon cocoa
1 cup butter-flavored vegetable oil
    and 1/2 cup regular vegetable oil
1-1/2 cups sugar

2 eggs
1 (1-ounce) bottle red food
    coloring
1 teaspoon vinegar
1 teaspoon vanilla extract
1 cup buttermilk

Sift dry ingredients together. Cream oil and sugar together until well blended. Add eggs one at a time, beating well after each addition. Add food coloring, vinegar, and vanilla extract; mix well. Add dry ingredients alternately with buttermilk. Bake in three greased and floured 9-inch round layer cake pans at 350°F for 25 minutes or until cakes test done. Cool completely and frost with **Cream Cheese Frosting**.

. . . .

red velvet cake no. 2

1 stick butter
1 cup vegetable oil
2 cups sugar
4 eggs
1 teaspoon vanilla extract
1 (1-ounce) bottle red food
  coloring

1 teaspoon vinegar
3 cups sifted cake flour
1 teaspoon baking soda
1-1/2 teaspoons cocoa
1 cup buttermilk

Cream butter, oil, and sugar together until very light and fluffy. Add eggs one at a
time, beating well after each addition. Add vanilla extract and blend well. Add food
coloring and vinegar and mix thoroughly. Add sifted dry ingredients alternately
with buttermilk. Bake in four greased and floured 9-inch layer cake pans at 350°F
for approximately 25 minutes or until cakes test done. Cool completely and frost
with **Cream Cheese Frosting**.

cream cheese frosting

1 stick butter
1 (8-ounce) package cream cheese, softened
1 (16-ounce) box confectioners sugar
1/2 teaspoon vanilla extract
1 cup chopped pecans

Cream butter and cream cheese well. Add confectioners sugar and vanilla extract,
blend well. Fold in pecans and spread on cooled cake.

raisin cake

1 (15-ounce) box raisins
2 cups sugar
1 cup butter
2 cups boiling water
2 tablespoons baking soda
1/4 cup warm water
2 eggs, slightly beaten

4-1/2 cups all-purpose flour
1/2 teaspoon baking powder
1 tablespoon ground allspice
2 teaspoons cinnamon
1 teaspoon ground cloves
2 cups chopped pecans or walnuts

Combine raisins, sugar, butter, and boiling water in a large saucepan; bring to a boil and boil for 5 minutes. Allow to cool to lukewarm.

Dissolve baking soda in warm water, add to raisin mixture. (Mixture will foam.) Stir in eggs. Combine dry ingredients; gradually add to raisin mixture, stirring well after each addition. Stir in pecans or walnuts, if desired.

Spoon batter into a lightly greased 10-inch bundt or tube pan. Bake at 350°F approximately 1 hour or until tests done.

. . . .

raspberry cake

1 cup butter
2 cups sugar
7 egg yolks, unbeaten
4 cups sifted cake flour
2-1/2 teaspoons baking powder
1/2 teaspoon salt

1/2 cup milk
2 tablespoons orange zest
4 tablespoons very finely shaved
  citron
7 egg whites, beaten stiff
Raspberry whipped cream

Cream butter thoroughly with sugar. Add egg yolks one at a time, beating well after each addition. To batter, alternately add sifted dry ingredients with milk and beat until smooth. Add zest and citron. Add to butter mixture and blend well. Fold egg whites into batter. Pour batter into three greased and floured 9-inch layer cake pans. Bake at 350°F for 25 to 30 minutes. Cool and spread with **Raspberry**

Whipped Cream between layers and over top and sides of cake. Sprinkle generously with very finely shaved citron.

. . . .

raspberry whipped cream

1 pint heavy sweet cream
3 tablespoons raspberry jelly

Beat cream until stiff peaks form. Fold in jelly, only once or twice, giving a marbled effect. Spread over cake immediately.

. . . .

scripture cake

1 cup Judges 5:25 (last clause)	**Butter**
2 cups Jeremiah 6:20	**Sugar**
Six of Jeremiah 17:11	**Eggs**
3-1/2 cups I Kings 4:22	**Flour**
2 teaspoons Amos 4:5 (leavening)	**Baking Powder**
Pinch of Leviticus 2:13	**Salt**
Season to taste with II Chronicles 9:19	**Spices***
1/2 cup Judges 4:19 (last clause)	**Milk**
2 tablespoons I Samuel 14:25	**Honey**
2 cups I Samuel 30:12	**Raisins**
2 cups Nahum 3:12	**Figs**
2 cups Numbers 17:8	**Almonds**

***1 tablespoon each of allspice, cinnamon, and nutmeg**

Cream together butter and sugar until light and very fluffy. Add eggs one at a time, beating well after each addition. Add sifted flour, baking powder, salt, and spices alternately with milk and honey. Dredge raisins and figs in a very small amount of flour and then stir in with very finely chopped almonds. Pour into a large greased and floured tube pan. Bake at 300°F for approximately 1 hour and 30 minutes or until tests done.

. . . .

silver cake (white cake)

3 cups sifted cake flour
3 teaspoons baking powder
1/2 cup butter
1-1/2 cups sugar

1 cup milk
1/2 teaspoon lemon extract
4 egg whites, stiffly beaten

Sift flour once, measure, add baking powder and sift together 3 times. Cream butter thoroughly, add sugar gradually, and cream together until light and fluffy. Add flour, alternately with milk, a small amount at a time, beating well after each addition until smooth. Add lemon extract. Fold in egg whites. Pour into three greased 9-inch layer cake pans. Bake at 350°F for 25 to 30 minutes. Spread with your favorite frosting.

. . . .

silhouette cake

Batter:

2-1/3 cups softed cake flour
2-1/4 teaspoons baking powder
1/4 teaspoon salt
1/2 cup butter
1 cup sugar

1 whole egg and 2 egg yolks, well
  beaten
1 teaspoon vanilla extract
3/4 cup milk

Chocolate Mixture:

2-1/2 ounces unsweetened
  chocolate, melted
1/2 teaspoon baking soda
3 tablespoons sugar

2 tablespoons butter, melted
1/4 teaspoon salt
1/4 cup boiling water

Sift flour once, measure; add baking powder and salt and sift together 3 times. Cream butter thoroughly; add sugar gradually, creaming until light and fluffy. Add whole egg and egg yolks and beat well after each addition. Add vanilla extract.

Prepare chocolate mixture by combining melted chocolate, baking soda, sugar, butter, salt, and water. Mix well. Put aside.

Add flour to first mixture alternately with milk, blending well after each addition. Pour 1/3 of batter into a greased 9-inch layer cake pan. Add chocolate mixture to remaining batter, blend, pour into two greased 9-inch layer cake pans. Bake all layers at 350°F for 20 to 25 minutes or until cakes test done. Frost with **Harvest Frosting**. Stack plain layer between chocolate layers.

harvest frosting

4 egg whites, unbeaten
2 cups firmly packed brown sugar
Pinch of salt
1/4 cup water

1 teaspoon vanilla extract
3/4 cup almonds, blanched,
  chopped, toasted

Combine egg whites, sugar, salt, and water in top of double boiler, beating with rotary beater until thoroughly mixed. Place over rapidly boiling water beating constantly, and cook for 7 minutes. Remove from heat, add vanilla extract and beat until thick enough to spread. Add nuts. You may also melt 2 additional squares of chocolate and pour over top of cake for decoration, if desired.

7 up® cake

4 eggs
3/4 cup vegetable oil
1 (10-ounce) bottle 7 Up
1 box instant pineapple pudding
1 box Lemon Supreme cake mix

Beat eggs thoroughly; add oil and blend. Add 7 Up, pudding, and cake mix and blend thoroughly. Pour batter into three greased and floured 9-inch layer cake pans. Bake at 350°F for approximately 30 minutes or until cakes test done. Cool layers completely and ice with **Pineapple Coconut Icing.**

pineapple coconut icing

1 cup crushed pineapple
1 stick butter
1 cup sugar
1 tablespoon flour

1 cup coconut flakes
1 teaspoon vanilla extract
1 cup chopped pecans

Combine all ingredients in a saucepan and cook for 5 minutes, stirring constantly. Spread on cooled cake layers.

. . . .

shortcakes

1-1/4 sticks butter
1/4 cup sugar
1-1/2 cups cake flour
Jelly
Confectioners sugar icing

Cream together butter, sugar, and flour. Roll out to 1/4-inch thickness on lightly floured board; cut in small rounds. Bake at 300°F until light brown. While still hot, stack 2 rounds, spreading your favorite jelly between layers. Ice with a confectioners sugar icing. Place a pecan half on top of each round, if desired.

. . . .

silver moon cake (white cake)

2/3 cup butter
1-3/4 cups sugar
3 cups sifted cake flour
1/2 teaspoon salt

3 teaspoons baking powder
1 cup milk
1 teaspoon vanilla extract
5 egg whites, stiffly beaten

Cream butter and sugar together until light and fluffy. Add sifted dry ingredients alternately with milk. Add vanilla extract. Fold in egg whites. Pour into three greased and floured 9-inch layer cake pans. Bake at 350°F for approximately 30 minutes. Spread with icing of your choice.

sock-it-to-me cake

Cake:

1 box butter cake mix
1 cup sour cream
1/2 cup vegetable oil
1/4 cup sugar
1/4 cup milk

4 eggs
1 cup chopped pecans
2 tablespoons brown sugar
2 teaspoons cinnamon

Glaze:

1 cup confectioners sugar
2 tablespoons milk

To prepare cake: Blend together cake mix, sour cream, oil, sugar, milk, and eggs. With electric mixer at high speed, beat for 2 minutes. Pour 2/3 of the batter into a greased and floured bundt or tube pan. Combine pecans, brown sugar, and cinnamon and sprinkle mixture over the batter. Spread remaining batter evenly into pan. Bake at 350°F for approximately 25 minutes. Drizzle glaze over cake
To prepare glaze: Blend confectioners sugar and milk together thoroughly.

sour cream cake

1/2 cup butter, softened	1-1/2 teaspoons baking soda
1-1/2 cups sugar	1 teaspoon salt
2 eggs	1-1/2 cups sour cream
3 cups sifted cake flour	1 teaspoon vanilla extract

Cream butter and sugar together until light and fluffy. Add eggs one at a time, beating well after each addition. Add sifted dry ingredients alternately with sour cream. Add vanilla extract. Pour batter into three greased and floured 9-inch layer cake pans. Bake at 350°F for 25 to 30 minutes or until cakes test done. Cool. Spread with **Strawberry Seven-Minute Frosting**.

strawberry seven-minute frosting

7 tablespoons strawberry pureé	Pinch of salt
2 egg whites	1-1/2 cups sugar
1 teaspoon cream of tartar	2 teaspoons white corn syrup

Combine first 5 ingredients in top of double boiler over boiling water. Beat with electric beater until mixture stands in peaks. Remove from heat. Replace hot water with cold, add syrup and beat until mixture is cool and stiff.

sour cream custard cake

Custard:
1 tablespoon cornstarch
2 tablespoons cold water
1 cup sour cream
1/2 cup sugar

Cake:

1-1/2 cups sifted cake flour
1/2 teaspoon salt
2 teaspoons baking powder
2/3 cup sugar
1/4 cup shortening, melted

1 egg, beaten
1/2 cup milk
1/2 teaspoon vanilla extract
1/2 teaspoon cinnamon

To prepare custard: Mix cornstarch and water to a smooth paste. Heat cream, adding 1/2 cup sugar and cornstarch mixture. Cook 15 minutes over low heat, stirring constantly. Cool.

To prepare cake: Lightly grease a 9-inch springform pan. Sift flour, salt, baking powder, and sugar together. Combine butter, egg, milk, vanilla extract. Add to dry ingredients, beating 1 minute until smooth. Pour into springform pan. Make an indentation in center of batter and pour custard into it slowly. Cake batter will be pushed toward edges of pan and custard will remain in center. (As it bakes, cake will rise partly over custard.) Sprinkle with cinnamon. Bake at 350°F for 25 minutes or until tests done.

- - - - - - - - -

sour cream fudge cake

2 cups sifted cake flour
1-1/2 cups sugar
1 teaspoon baking soda
1 teaspoon salt
1/3 cup solid shortening
1 cup sour cream

3 ounces unsweetened chocolate, melted
2 eggs
1 teaspoon vanilla extract
1/4 cup hot water

Sift flour, sugar, baking soda, and salt together. Cut in shortening, then add sour cream, beating 2 minutes. Add remaining ingredients, beating an additional 2 minutes.

Grease the bottom of a 13 x 9 x 1-1/2-inch pan; line with wax paper, then grease the paper. Pour batter into pan. Bake at 350°F for 25 to 30 minutes. Cool cake in pan for 5 minutes. Turn out onto wire rack and remove wax paper. Frost as desired, serving in squares. This cake is especially good with a **Seven-Minute Frosting**.

- - - - - - - -

sponge cake

6 eggs, separated
1/4 cup water
1 teaspoon vanilla extract
1/2 teaspoon salt
1 cup sugar

1-1/2 cups cake flour
1/2 teaspoon baking powder
1 teaspoon cream of tartar
1/2 cup sugar

With electric mixer at high speed, beat egg yolks until thick and lemon colored. Add water and vanilla extract and blend well. Beat until thoroughly blended and thickened; then gradually beat in salt and 1 cup sugar. Sift flour and baking powder together. Sprinkle approximately 1/4 at a time over yolk mixture and carefully fold in; set aside.

Beat egg whites until foamy and add cream of tartar, beating until soft peaks form. Gradually add 1/2 cup sugar, 2 tablespoons at a time, beating until stiff peaks form. Gently fold egg whites into yolk mixture. Pour batter into an ungreased 10-inch tube pan. Bake at 350°F for 50 minutes or until tests done.

Remove from oven and invert pan. Cool completely before removing from pan.

. . . .

spice cake

1-1/2 cups boiling water
1 cup quick-cooking rolled oats
1/2 cup shortening
1/2 cup sugar
1 cup firmly packed brown sugar
2 eggs
1 teaspoon vanilla extract

1-1/2 cups sifted flour
1 teaspoon cinnamon
1/2 teaspoon salt
1 teaspoon baking soda
1 teaspoon nutmeg
1/4 teaspoon allspice
1/2 cup chopped walnuts or pecans

Pour water over oats; let stand until cool.

Mix together shortening and sugars until light and fluffy. Beat in eggs one at a time, beating well after each addition. Stir in oat mixture and vanilla extract. Mix in dry ingredients. Sift together all dry ingredients except nuts and add to batter.

Blend well. Stir in nuts. Spread mixture in greased and floured 9-inch square pan. Bake at 350°F for 45 to 50 minutes. Cool in pan on wire rack. Spread with **Lemon Butter Frosting**.

lemon butter frosting

1/4 cup butter
1/4 cup shortening
2 cups confectioners sugar
1 tablespoon milk

1 teaspoon grated lemon zest
1/2 teaspoon lemon extract
Pinch of salt

Cream together butter and shortening. Gradually beat in confectioners sugar. Add milk, zest, lemon extract, and salt. Whip until light and creamy.

spice surprise cake

2 cups sifted flour
1/2 cup cocoa
2 teaspoons baking powder
1/2 teaspoon salt
1 teaspoon cinnamon
1 teaspoon ground cloves
1 teaspoon nutmeg
1 cup butter

2 cups sugar
4 eggs
1 cup unseasoned mashed potatoes
1/2 cup whipping cream
1 (8-1/2-ounce) can crushed
    pineapple, drained
1 cup chopped pecans

Sift flour, cocoa, baking powder, salt, and spices together.

Cream butter and sugar until light and fluffy. Add eggs one at a time, beating well after each addition. Beat in mashed potatoes. Add dry ingredients alternately with cream, beating well after each addition. Stir in pineapple and pecans. Pour into a greased and floured 13 x 9 x 2-inch cake pan. Bake at 350°F for approximately 45 minutes. Cool in pan on wire rack. Frost with **Cream Cheese Frosting**.

cream cheese frosting

1 (8-ounce) package cream cheese
1/4 cup butter
2 cups sifted confectioners sugar
2 teaspoons vanilla extract

Beat together cream cheese and butter. Slowly beat in confectioners sugar and vanilla extract; beat until light and fluffy.

. . . .

strawberry cake

2 sticks butter
2 cups sugar
1 small package strawberry gelatin
3-1/2 cups sifted cake flour

3 teaspoons baking powder
1 cup milk
1/2 cup strawberries, cut up
6 egg whites, stiffly beaten

Preheat oven to 350°F. Cream together butter, sugar, and gelatin until light and fluffy. Add sifted flour and baking powder alternately with milk. Fold in strawberries. Fold in egg whites. Pour into three or four greased and floured 9-inch round cake pans. Bake at 350°F approximately 25 minutes or until tests done. Spread **Strawberry Icing** between layers and on top and sides.

strawberry icing

1 stick butter, softened
1/2 cup strawberries, cut up
1 (16-ounce) box confectioners sugar

Blend all ingredients well and spread on cake when cool.

. . . .

spice caramel cake

1-3/4 cups sugar
1 cup cold mashed potatoes
3/4 cup soft shortening
3 eggs
2-1/4 cups flour
1 teaspoon baking soda

1 teaspoon cinnamon
1/2 teaspoon salt
1/2 teaspoon nutmeg
1 cup buttermilk
3/4 cup chopped pecans

Preheat oven 350°F. Combine sugar, potatoes, and shortening. Cream well. Add eggs one at a time, beating well after each addition. Sift dry ingredients together and add alternately with buttermilk beginning and ending with flour mixture. Add pecans. Pour into a greased and floured 13 x 9 x 2-inch pan. Bake at 350°F for 50 minutes to 1 hour. Cool and frost with **Quick Caramel Frosting**.

quick caramel frosting

1/4 cup butter
3/4 cup firmly packed brown sugar
3 tablespoons milk
2 cups confectioners sugar

Melt butter in saucepan. Stir in brown sugar. Continue cooking over low heat for 2 minutes. Add milk. Bring to a full boil; cool to lukewarm without stirring. Add confectioners sugar. Beat until smooth and of spreading consistency.

spice sour cream cake

1 cup butter, softened
1 cup sugar
6 eggs, separated
1 cup molasses

4 cups all-purpose flour
1 teaspoon salt
1 teaspoon allspice
1 teaspoon ground cloves

1 teaspoon cinnamon
1 teaspoon nutmeg
8 ounces sour cream

1 teaspoon baking soda
Confectioners sugar

Cream butter and sugar together until light and fluffy. Add egg yolks one at a time, beating well after each addition. Add molasses and beat well.

Sift flour, salt, and spices together. Combine sour cream and baking soda and mix well. Add flour mixture to creamed mixture alternately with sour cream mixture, beginning and ending with flour mixture.

Beat egg whites until stiff peaks form; gently fold into batter. Pour into a greased and floured 10-inch tube pan. Bake at 300°F for 1 hour and 40 minutes or until tests done. Cool in pan for 10 minutes; remove from pan and cool completely. Sprinkle with confectioners sugar.

strawberry meringue cake

1/2 cup sugar
1/2 cup butter
4 egg yolks
2-1/2 cups sifted flour
1 teaspoon baking powder
1/4 teaspoon salt
1/4 cup milk

4 egg whites
1 cup sugar
1 tablespoon vanilla extract
Chopped pecans
Strawberries
Sweetened whipped cream

Cream 1/2 cup sugar and butter; add beaten yolks; beat until light and fluffy. Sift flour, baking powder, and salt; add to mixture alternately with milk. Pour into greased long cake pan; set aside in cool place.

Beat egg whites; add 1 cup sugar gradually until soft peaks form. Beat in vanilla extract. Spread onto cake batter; sprinkle with chopped pecans. Bake at 325°F for 20 to 25 minutes. Cool. Put fresh strawberries on top. Serve with sweetened whipped cream.

strawberry shortcake

2 cups all-purpose flour
3 teaspoons baking powder
1/2 teaspoon salt
1/2 cup sugar
1/2 cup butter

3/4 cup milk or light cream
1 quart strawberries, halved and
   sweetened to taste
1 cup whipping cream, whipped and
   sweetened

Sift flour, baking powder, salt, and sugar together. Cut in butter until mixture resembles coarse breadcrumbs. Stir in milk. (Don't overmix.) Turn dough out onto floured board, knead quickly to distribute ingredients evenly.

With floured rolling pin, roll out dough approximately 3/4-inch thick. Cut into rounds with a 3-inch cookie cutter or the open end of a drinking glass dipped in flour. Place 2 inches apart on ungreased cookie sheet. Bake at 400°F for approximately 10 to 15 minutes or until golden brown. Split crosswise while warm, butter both halves. Spoon sweetened berries over bottom layer; cover with top layer, and spoon more strawberries on top. Top each with whipped cream and a whole berry.

. . . .

strawberry cream cake

2 (10-ounce) packages frozen strawberries or 1 quart fresh strawberries, sweetened and sliced
2 cups all-purpose flour
1 teaspoon baking powder
1/2 teaspoon baking soda
1/2 teaspoon salt
1-1/4 cups sugar

1 cup butter, softened
2 eggs
8 ounces sour cream
1/3 cup firmly packed light brown
   sugar
1/2 cup chopped pecans
1 teaspoon cinnamon

Drain strawberries and reserve juice for glaze. Sift flour, baking powder, baking soda, and salt together; set aside.

Combine 1-1/4 cups sugar and butter in a large mixing bowl, creaming well. Add eggs, beating until smooth. Slowly mix in sour cream. Add flour mixture and stir in well.

Combine brown sugar, pecans, and cinnamon; set aside for topping. Pour 1/2 of batter into a lightly greased 13 x 9 x 2-inch baking pan. Spoon strawberries over batter; sprinkle with half of topping mixture. Top with remaining batter and sprinkle with remaining topping. Bake at 350°F for 30 to 35 minutes or until tests done. Cool; cut into approximately 15 squares. Top each square with **Strawberry Glaze** and sweetened whipped cream.

strawberry glaze

Juice reserved from 2 (10-ounce) packages frozen strawberries or 1 quart fresh sliced strawberries
1 teaspoon cornstarch
2 teaspoons freshly squeezed lemon juice

Combine strawberry juice and cornstarch in a small saucepan; cook over medium heat, stirring constantly until thickened. Remove from heat and stir in lemon juice. Serve warm over cake.

strawberry sponge cake

Cake:
1 cup flour
1 teaspoon baking powder
5 eggs
3/4 cup sugar
5 tablespoons butter
1/4 cup heavy cream
2 teaspoons grated lemon peel
1 teaspoon lemon extract
1 teaspoon vanilla extract

Filling and Topping:

1 quart strawberries, hulled and halved (reserve a few whole and unhulled for garnish)

1/2 cup sugar

1-1/2 cups heavy cream, whipped

To prepare cake: Sift flour and baking powder together; set aside. Beat eggs and sugar together in large mixing bowl. In small saucepan over low heat melt butter in cream; set aside to cool slightly. Fold flour mixture into egg mixture. Fold in cream mixture, peel, and extracts. Bake in two greased and floured 9-inch layer cake pans at 350°F for 20 to 25 minutes.

To prepare filling and topping: Gently toss berries with sugar. Let stand at room temperature until juice forms (approximately 1 hour). Place 1 layer of cake on serving plate. Spoon 1/2 quart berries and juice over the layer; top with whipped cream. Place second layer of cake on top, then top with remaining berries and juice. Mound remaining whipped cream in center. Garnish with whole berries.

vanilla wafer cake

2 sticks butter
2 cups sugar
6 eggs
1 (12-ounce) box vanilla wafers

1/2 cup milk
1 (7-ounce) can flake coconut
1 cup chopped pecans

Cream butter and sugar until light and fluffy. Add eggs one at a time, beating well after each addition. Crush wafers with a rolling pin until crumbs are fine. Add wafer crumbs and milk alternately to creamed mixture. Add coconut, then fold in pecans. Pour batter into a greased and floured tube pan. Bake at 300°F for 1 hour and 15 minutes or until tests done. Cool in pan before removing.

sugar plum cake

3/4 cup butter
1-3/4 cups sugar
4 eggs
4 cups flour
3/4 pound candied orange slices, cut
    finely with kitchen scissors
1-1/2 cups coarsely chopped pecans
1 (8-ounce) package dates, cut
    small

1 (3-1/2-ounce) can flaked coconut
1/8 teaspoon salt
1 teaspoon baking soda
2/3 cup buttermilk
1 tablespoon lemon juice
1 teaspoon orange extract

Preheat oven to 300°F. Cream butter and sugar until light and fluffy. Add eggs one at a time, beating well after each addition. Sift 1/2 cup flour over orange candy, pecans, dates, and coconut; mix well.

Sift remaining flour with salt and baking soda. Add alternately with buttermilk. Stir in lemon juice and orange extract. With hands, mix in dredged fruits. Pour batter into two greased and floured 9 x 5 x 3-inch loaf pans. Bake at 300°F for 1 hour and 40 minutes. Start testing for doneness after 1 hour and 15 minutes. Let cake rest for 5 minutes, then prick all over with skewer or ice pick and spoon **Orange Glaze** over cake.

orange glaze

2 cups confectioners sugar
2 teaspoons grated orange zest
1 cup orange juice

Blend all ingredients together thoroughly.

. . . .

sweet potato cake

1-1/2 cups vegetable oil
2 cups sugar
4 eggs, separated
4 tablespoons hot water
2-1/2 cups cake flour
3 teaspoons baking powder
1/4 teaspoon salt

1 teaspoon cinnamon
1 teaspoon nutmeg
1-1/2 cups grated raw sweet potatoes
1 cup chopped pecans
1 teaspoon vanilla extract
Coconut Filling

Combine oil and sugar in a large mixing bowl and beat until smooth. Add egg yolks and beat well. Stir in hot water. Sift dry ingredients together; blend into sugar mixture, continuing to mix thoroughly. Stir in potatoes, pecans, and vanilla extract. Beat egg whites until stiff peaks form; fold into batter.

Spoon mixture into three greased 8-inch layer cake pans. Bake at 350°F for 25 to 30 minutes. Remove from pans; cool and spread **Coconut Filling** between layers and on top of cake. Garnish with whole pecans, if desired.

coconut filling

1 (13-ounce) can evaporated milk
1 cup sugar
1/2 cup butter
3 tablespoons flour
1 teaspoon vanilla extract
1 (3-1/2-ounce) can flaked coconut

Combine milk, sugar, butter, flour, and vanilla extract in a saucepan. Cook, stirring constantly, over medium heat; stir in coconut. Beat until thickened and cooled.

· · · · · · · ·

tropical chiffon cake

2-1/4 cups sifted cake flour
3 teaspoons baking powder
3/4 teaspoon salt
1-1/2 cups sugar
1/2 cup vegetable oil

6 large eggs, separated
2 large ripe bananas, sieved
1-1/2 teaspoons grated orange zest
1/3 cup orange juice
1/2 teaspoon cream of tartar

Sift dry ingredients into mixing bowl. Make well in center of dry ingredients and fill with oil, egg yolks, bananas, zest, and juice. Beat mixture with a wooden spoon until smooth.

Put egg whites in large bowl, add cream of tartar and beat until peaks are formed. Fold into batter, mixing well. Pour into ungreased 10-inch tube pan. Bake at 325°F for approximately 1 hour and 10 minutes. Invert pan and cool completely. Frost with your favorite cream cheese frosting or a glaze.

walnut cake

1 cup butter
2 cups sugar
5 eggs
1 teaspoon vanilla extract
3-1/2 cups sifted cake flour

1 tablespoon baking powder
1/2 teaspoon salt
1 cup milk
2 cups chopped walnuts

Cream butter and sugar until light and fluffy. Add eggs one at a time, beating well after each addition. Add vanilla extract and blend well. Add sifted dry ingredients alternately with milk. Stir in walnuts. Pour into two lightly greased loaf pans. Bake at 350°F for approximately 45 to 50 minutes. Cool. Spread with **Chocolate Nut Frosting**.

chocolate nut frosting

2 (1-ounce) squares unsweetened
  chocolate
2 tablespoons strong brewed coffee
5 egg yolks

1 cup sugar
1/4 teaspoon salt
1 cup butter
1 cup chopped walnuts

Melt chocolate in very hot coffee, stirring often; set aside. Beat egg yolks until light lemon color, then add sugar and salt and beat until smooth. Spoon chocolate mixture into yolk mixture. Add butter and cook over medium heat until mixture thickens slightly and becomes spreading consistency. Add nuts and spread over cake immediately.

walnut coconut cake

1/2 cup butter
1/2 cup shortening
2 cups sugar
5 eggs, separated
2-1/2 cups cake flour
1 teaspoon baking soda

1 cup buttermilk
1 teaspoon vanilla extract
1-1/2 cups chopped walnuts
1 (3-1/2-ounce) can flaked coconut
1/2 teaspoon cream of tartar

Cream butter and shortening; gradually add sugar, beating until light and fluffy. Add egg yolks one at a time, beating well after each addition. Add sifted dry ingredients alternately with buttermilk. Stir in vanilla extract. Add chopped walnuts and coconut, blending well. Beat egg whites with cream of tartar until stiff peaks form. Fold egg whites into batter. Pour batter into three greased and floured 9-inch round cake pans. Bake at 350°F for 30 minutes or until tests done. Cool completely. Frost with **Cream Cheese Frosting** and sprinkle with chopped walnuts.

cream cheese frosting

3/4 cup butter, softened.
1 (3-ounce) package cream cheese, softened
1 (8-ounce) package cream sugar cheese, softened
6-3/4 cups confectioners sugar
1-1/2 teaspoons vanilla extract

Cream butter and cream cheese; gradually add sugar, beating until light and creamy. Stir in vanilla extract.

. . . .

walnut torte

6 eggs, separated
1 cup sugar
3-1/2 tablespoons cake flour
1 teaspoon baking powder
1/2 teaspoon salt

3-1/4 cups ground walnuts
1 cup whipping cream, whipped and
   sweetened
1 tablespoon chopped walnuts

Beat egg yolks and sugar until thick and lemon colored. Sift together flour, baking powder, and salt. Using an electric mixer on medium speed, gradually add flour mixture to batter and continue beating until well blened, approximately 4 minutes. Beat egg whites until stiff peaks form. Gently fold ground walnuts into egg whites, then gently fold in the egg yolk mixture.

Grease two 8-inch layer cake pans, line with wax paper and grease again. Pour batter into pans. Bake at 350°F for 25 to 30 minutes. Cool cakes in pans on wire racks for 5 minutes. Remove from pans and gently remove wax paper. Cool cakes completely and spread top of cakes with whipped cream and chopped nuts.

. . . .

zucchini chocolate cake

1/2 cup butter
1/2 cup vegetable oil
1-3/4 cups sugar
2 eggs
2-1/2 cups cake flour
1 teaspoon baking powder
1/2 salt

1/3 cup cocoa
1 teaspoon baking soda
1/2 cup sour milk (put l tablespoon
   vinegar in cup, add milk to 1/2
   cup line)
1 cup chopped pecans
2 cups grated raw zucchini

Beat together butter and oil. Add sugar and blend well. Add 2 beaten eggs and beat well. Sift flour, baking powder, salt, cocoa, and baking soda together. Add dry ingredients to batter alternately with sour milk, beating well after each addition. Stir into batter by hand the pecans and grated zucchini. Pour batter in greased and floured bundt or tube pan or two loaf pans. Bake at 325°F for 45 to 50 minutes.

. . . .

zucchini cake

1 cup vegetable oil
2 cups sugar
3 eggs, beaten
2-1/2 cups cake flour
2 teaspoons baking soda

1/2 teaspoon baking powder
1/2 teaspoon salt
3 teaspoons cinnamon
2 cups grated raw zucchini
1 tablespoon vanilla extract

Beat oil and sugar until well blended. Add beaten eggs and blend thoroughly. Add sifted remaining dry ingredients, mixing well. Stir in zucchini and vanilla extract. Pour batter into a greased and floured 10-inch bundt or tube pan. Bake at 350°F for 55 to 60 minutes. Cool before removing from pan.

Pour **Confectioner's Sugar Glaze** over top.

confectioners sugar glaze

1 cup confectioners sugar
3 teaspoons milk

Combine and mix well, gradually adding enough milk to make a glaze.

. . . .

washington cake

1 pound butter
2 cups sugar
8 eggs
4-1/2 cups cake flour
1 teaspoon each of cinnamon and
**   ground cloves, mixed**

1 pound raisins, chopped fine
1 pound currants
1 nutmeg, grated
1/2 cup whipping cream
1/4 cup wine

Cream butter and sugar together until light and fluffy. Add eggs one at a time, beating well after each addition. Add sifted remaining dry ingredients alternately with cream and wine. Pour batter into a large, lightly greased tube pan. Bake at 300°F for approximately 1 hour and 30 minutes. Serve plain or with your favorite glaze.

. . . .

angel
food cakes

Nothing can compare to the wonderful aroma of a cake baking.

angel food cake

1-1/3 cups sugar
1 cup cake flour
1/2 teaspoon salt
1-1/2 cups egg whites (approximately 12)

1-1/4 teaspoons cream of tartar
1 teaspoon vanilla extract
1/2 teaspoon almond extract

Preheat oven to 350°F. Sift 1/4 cup sugar, cake flour, and salt together. Sift mixture 3 times. With an electric mixer, beat egg whites until foamy. Add cream of tartar. Continue beating until egg whites hold soft peaks. While still beating, gradually add remaining sugar, 1 tablespoon at a time. Fold in vanilla extract and almond extract. Sift approximately 1/4 of the flour mixture over batter and fold into batter using a rubber spatula. Continue adding flour mixture 1/4 at a time; fold in after each addition.

Pour batter into an ungreased tube pan. Bake 45 minutes or until top of cake springs back when lightly touched.

Immediately turn the pan upside down, suspending if necessary, the tube part over the neck of a funnel or bottle. Let the cake stand in the pan until cool, approximately 1-1/2 hours.

filling for angel food cake

1 package instant vanilla pudding
1 envelope gelatin (unflavored)
3/4 cup sugar
1 (15-1/4-ounce) can peaches, mashed and drained; or 1 (8-1/4-ounce) pineapple, drained
1 pint whipping cream, whipped

Slice an angel food cake into 3 layers. Mix all dry ingredients together; add fruit and let stand while whipping cream. Fold whipped cream into mixture and spread between layers of angel food cake.

heavenly topping for angel food cake

1 pint vanilla ice cream
1 cup crushed pineapple, drained
1 cup sliced ripe strawberries
1/4 cup chopped pecans
1 cup miniature marshmallows
1 package whipped topping, whipped; or 1 pint whipping cream, whipped

Split an angel food cake into 2 layers and place a layer of ice cream between them. Return top layer, wrap in foil and freeze.

Combine fruits, nuts, and marshmallows; fold into whipped topping and chill at least 2 hours. To serve, slice cake and spread with topping. Looks pretty if topped with a maraschino cherry or a halved strawberry.

mocha angel food cake

1 cup sifted cake flour
2 cups sugar
1/2 cup unsweetened cocoa
1 tablespoon instant coffee
1-1/2 cups egg whites (from 12 large eggs)
1/2 teaspoon salt
1-1/2 teaspoons cream of tartar
1-1/2 teaspoons vanilla extract

Sift together cake flour, 1 cup sugar, cocoa, and coffee. Beat egg whites, salt, and cream of tartar together until whites hold straight peaks. Add remaining 1 cup sugar and vanilla extract and beat until whites hold soft peaks. Gradually fold in flour mixture until blended. Pour into an ungreased 10-inch angel food cake pan. Bake at 375°F for 35 minutes or until tests done. If top browns too much toward end of baking period, cover loosely with foil. Invert pan and cool for 1 hour. Loosen edges and ease from pan. Cut in 3 layers with a serrated knife. Fill and frost with **Mocha Cream**. Refrigerate.

mocha cream

- 2 cups heavy cream
- 1 cup instant cocoa mix
- 2 tablespoons instant coffee granules

Whip together cream, cocoa mix, and instant coffee granules until cream is stiff.

. . . .

marble angel food cake

- 3/4 cup sifted cake flour
- 1/2 cup sugar
- 1-1/4 cups egg whites (9 to 11 medium)
- 1/4 teaspoon salt
- 1-1/4 teaspoons cream of tartar

- 3/4 cup sugar
- 1 teaspoon vanilla extract
- 1/4 teaspoon almond extract
- 2 tablespoons cake flour
- 2 tablespoons sugar
- 3 tablespoons cocoa

Sift flour and 1/2 cup sugar together. Beat egg whites, salt, and cream of tartar until foamy. Sprinkle 3/4 cup sugar, 2 tablespoons at a time, over egg whites, beating well after each addition. Continue beating until stiff straight peaks form. Add vanilla extract and almond extract. Sift in dry ingredients gradually, folding carefully but thoroughly. Divide batter in half. Sift 2 tablespoons cake flour and 2 tablespoons sugar together; fold into half of batter. Sift cocoa and 2 tablespoons sugar together; fold into remaining batter. Pour light and dark batters alternately into ungreased 9-inch tube pan. Bake at 325°F for 50 minutes to 1 hour. Cool in inverted pan for 1 hour.

. . . .

chocolate angel food cake

3/4 cup sifted cake flour
4 tablespoons cocoa
1-1/4 cups sifted sugar
1-1/4 cups egg whites
1/4 teaspoon salt
1 teaspoon cream of tartar
1 teaspoon vanilla extract

Sift flour, cocoa, and sugar together 6 times. Beat egg whites until foamy; add salt and cream of tartar and continue beating until eggs form stiff peaks but are not dry. Fold in vanilla extract. Sift 2 or 3 tablespoons dry ingredients at a time over egg whites and fold in lightly until all dry ingredients are used. Bake at 350°F for 50 to 1 hour and 10 minutes. Invert pan and let cake hang in pan until cool.

. . . .

chocolate pecan
angel food cake

2 cups sugar
1/4 teaspoon salt
1/2 cup cocoa
1 cup cake flour
1-1/2 cups egg whites (around 11 egg whites)
1 teaspoon cream of tartar
1 teaspoon vanilla extract
1 cup finely chopped pecans

Sift sugar, salt, cocoa, and flour together 5 times; set aside. With an electric mixer, beat egg whites until foamy. Add cream of tartar and then beat on highest speed until egg whites form very stiff peaks, but are not dry. Fold in flour mixture very gradually, blending well. Gently stir in vanilla extract. Pour 1/4 of the batter into an ungreased angel food cake pan. Sprinkle 1/3 of the pecans over top. Pour 1/4 of the batter over pecans. Repeat steps, ending with batter. Bake at 325°F for 1 hour or until top of cake springs back when lightly touched. Immediately invert pan and cool completely. Loosen edges and ease from pan.

meringue angel food cake

1-1/2 cups sugar
1/2 cup water
1-1/4 cups egg whites
1 teaspoon cream of tartar

1/4 teaspoon salt
1 teaspoon vanilla extract
1/4 teaspoon almond extract
1 cup sifted cake flour

Cook sugar and water to 242°F or until syrup spins a long thread. Beat egg whites until frothy. Add cream of tartar with salt and continue beating until egg whites form a stiff peak. Pour syrup slowly over egg whites and continue beating until mixture is cool. Add extracts. Fold in flour. Pour into an ungreased tube pan. Cut through batter with spatula to remove large air bubbles. Bake at 350°F for 45 minutes. Invert pan and let hang in pan until cool.

. . . .

angel ginger cake

2 cups sifted cake flour
1 teaspoon baking soda
1 teaspoon ground ginger
1/4 teaspoon salt
6 tablespoons butter

1/2 cup sugar
1/2 cup molasses
2 eggs, well beaten
1/2 cup buttermilk

Sift flour, soda, ginger, and salt together 3 times. Cream butter with sugar until fluffy. Add molasses, eggs, and milk and beat well. Fold in sifted dry ingredients thoroughly and pour into greased 8 x 10 x 2-inch pan. Bake at 350°F for 35 to 40 minutes.

. . . .

angel custard cake

- 6 egg yolks, beaten
- 3/4 cup sugar
- 3/4 cup freshly squeezed lemon juice
- 1/2 teaspoon grated lemon zest
- 1 tablespoon unflavored gelatin
- 1/4 cup water
- 6 egg whites, beaten
- 1 large angel food cake, torn into bite-size pieces

Combine egg yolks, 3/4 cup sugar, lemon juice, and lemon zest. Cook over hot, but not boiling, water until custard coats a spoon. Remove from heat; add gelatin, softened in 1/4 cup water, and stir until gelatin is dissolved. Fold in egg whites, beaten with remaining 3/4 cup sugar. Put angel food cake pieces in tube pan, oiled with salad oil. Pour custard over cake. Chill until firm; unmold. Fill center with whipped cream. Garnish with fresh cherries or maraschino cherries and green gumdrops, if desired.

. . . .

angel lemon cake

- 2 envelopes unflavored gelatin
- 1 cup lemon juice
- 6 large eggs, separated
- 2 cups sugar, divided
- 1 angel food cake, cut into bite-size pieces
- 1 cup whipping cream
- 1/4 cup confectioners sugar
- Yellow food coloring

Soften gelatin in lemon juice and let stand 5 minutes.

Beat egg yolks until thickened. Combine yolks, 1 cup sugar, and gelatin in a small saucepan and cook over low heat until thick; set aside to cool.

Beat egg whites until soft peaks form. Gradually add 1 cup sugar and continue beating until peaks are stiff and glossy. Fold gelatin mixture into egg whites.

Gently fold angel food cake pieces into gelatin mixture, coating all pieces well. Spoon into a lightly greased 10-inch tube pan; chill overnight.

Remove cake from pan by gently running knife between sides of cake and edge of pan; invert onto cake plate.

Combine whipping cream and confectioners sugar; beat until soft peaks form. Add a few drops of yellow food coloring, mixing well. Spread on top and sides of cake. Refrigerate until serving.

angel ice cream cake

1 angel food cake
1 quart strawberry ice cream, softened
1 pint vanilla ice cream, softened
2 cups whipping cream
1/4 cup confectioners sugar
1/4 teaspoon almond extract
1/4 cup slivered almonds, toasted

Cut cake into 4 layers. Place bottom layer of cake on a cake plate and spread with half of the strawberry ice cream; freeze. Add second layer and spread with vanilla ice cream; freeze. Repeat with third layer and remaining strawberry ice cream. Place remaining layer, cut side down, on top of cake. Cover and freeze cake several hours or overnight.

Beat whipping cream until foamy; gradually add confectioners sugar and almond extract, beating until stiff peaks form. Frost sides and top of cake with whipped cream. Sprinkle with toasted almonds, if desired.

angel sherry pudding cake

2 tablespoons unflavored gelatin
2-1/2 cups milk
3 eggs, separated
1/2 cup sugar
1/2 cup sherry
1/8 teaspoon salt
1 cup heavy cream, whipped
1 cup torn pieces of either angel food cake or ladyfingers

Dissolve gelatin in 1/2 cup milk; let stand 5 minutes. Mix egg yolks, sugar, salt, and remaining milk; cook over low heat until thick. Remove from heat; stir in dissolved gelatin and sherry; mix well. Cool. Beat egg whites until stiff peaks form. Pour cooled mixture over egg whites. Just before mixture begins to set, fold in whipped cream and cake pieces. Put into individual compotes or large mold. Refrigerate until serving.

. . . .

cheese
cakes

Ohs and *ahs* are sure to greet you when you bake one of these cakes.

almond cheesecake

Crust:
2 cups almonds
2 teaspoons butter, melted
4 tablespoons brown sugar
1/2 teaspoon vanilla extract
1 tablespoon water

Filling:
2 (8-ounce) packages cream cheese
3 eggs
2/3 cup sugar
1/8 teaspoon almond extract
3 tablespoons milk

Topping:
2 cups sour cream
3/4 cup sugar
2 teaspoons vanilla extract

To prepare crust: Grind almonds in food processor until fine; add butter, brown sugar, vanilla extract, and water while processor is going. Continue processing until mixture begins to fall from side of bowl. Press into a 9-inch pie pan.

To prepare filling: Beat cheese until light and creamy. Add eggs one at a time, beating after each addition. Add sugar and almond extract. Beat until thick and lemon colored (approximately 5 minutes). Add milk, blending well. Pour into unbaked pie crust. Bake at 325°F for 50 minutes. Cool for 20 minutes.

To prepare topping: Beat sour cream, sugar, and vanilla extract together. Spoon over cheesecake and spread smooth. Sprinkle with sliced almonds. Bake at 325°F for 15 minutes. Cool 8 hours or overnight before serving.

. . . .

fabulous cheesecake

Crust:
2 cups graham cracker crumbs
2 tablespoons sugar
1/2 cup butter, softened

Filling:

2 (8-ounce) packages cream cheese

1 (16-ounce) container cottage
  cheese

1-1/2 cups sugar

4 eggs, slightly beaten

3 tablespoons cornstarch

3 tablespoons flour

2 tablespoons lemon juice

1 teaspoon vanilla extract

1/2 pound butter, melted

1 pint sour cream

To prepare crust: Combine graham cracker crumbs, 2 tablespoons sugar, and butter. Press into bottom of greased springform pan.

To prepare filling: Beat cream cheese and cottage cheese until smooth and creamy. Gradually beat in sugar, then beat in 1 egg at a time until well combined. With electric mixer at low speed, beat in cornstarch, flour, lemon juice, and vanilla extract. Add melted butter and sour cream, beating just until smooth. Bake at 325°F for 1 hour and 10 minutes or until firm around the edges. Turn off oven; allow cake to cool completely in oven for 2 hours. Remove from oven and continue cooling; chill 8 hours or overnight.

Serve with fresh, sweetened berries, peaches, or pineapple, if desired.

. . . .

cherry cheesecake

Crust:

1 cup graham cracker crumbs

3 tablespoons sugar

3 tablespoons butter, melted

1/4 teaspoon cinnamon

Filling:

3 (8-ounce) packages cream cheese,
  softened

2 teaspoons lemon juice

1 cup sugar

5 eggs

1/4 teaspoon salt

Topping

1-1/2 cups sour cream

2 tablespoons sugar

1/2 teaspoon vanilla extract

1 (21-ounce) can cherry pie filling

To prepare crust: Combine graham cracker crumbs, 3 tablespoons sugar, butter, and cinnamon; mix well. Press into a 10-inch springform pan; set aside.

To prepare filling: Beat cream cheese and lemon juice in a large mixing bowl until soft and creamy. Add 1 cup sugar and mix well. Add eggs one at a time, mixing well after each addition. Add salt and beat with electric mixer on medium speed for 10 minutes. Pour mixture into crust and bake at 350°F for 45 minutes. Remove to wire rack and let stand for 20 minutes.

To prepare topping: Combine sour cream, 2 tablespoons sugar, and vanilla extract; stir well. Spread over cheesecake. Bake at 350°F for 10 minutes; cool. Chill 8 hours or overnight before removing sides from pan. Top with cherry pie filling.

. . . .

cheesecake

Crust:

1-1/2 cups graham cracker crumbs
2 tablespoons butter
2 tablespoons sugar

Filling:

1/2 cup sugar
2 tablespoons flour
1/4 teaspoon salt
2 (8-ounce) packages cream cheese
1 teaspoon vanilla extract
4 egg yolks
1 cup whipping cream
4 egg whites

To prepare crust: Blend graham cracker crumbs with butter and 2 tablespoons sugar. Press into bottom of springform pan.

To prepare filling: Blend 1/2 cup sugar with flour, salt, and cream cheese, mixing well. Add vanilla extract, stir in egg yolks and mix well. Add cream slowly and blend thoroughly. Beat egg whites until stiff peaks form. Fold in egg whites and pour mixture into crumb crust. Bake at 325°F for approximately 1 hour and 15 minutes or until center is set.

When cooled, spread with sweetened whipped cream, if desired.

. . . .

larry's famous cheesecake

Crust:
1-1/2 cups graham cracker crumbs
2 tablespoons sugar
1/4 cup, plus 2 tablespoons melted
   butter
1-1/2 teaspoons cinnamon

Filling:
3 (8-ounce) packages cream cheese,
   softened
1 cup sugar
4 eggs
6 to 7 tablespoons milk

Topping:
1 pint sour cream
3/4 cup sugar
1 teaspoon vanilla extract

To prepare crust: Combine crumbs, 2 tablespoons sugar, butter, and cinnamon, mixing well. Press into a 10-inch springform pan; set aside.

To prepare filling: Beat cream cheese in a large mixing bowl until soft and creamy. Gradually add 1 cup sugar, beating until soft and fluffy. Add eggs one at a time, beating well after each addition. Add 6 to 7 tablespoons milk and blend well. Pour mixture into crust; bake at 350°F for 25 to 35 minutes or until cake is set. Let cool for approximately 30 minutes.

To prepare topping: Beat sour cream and add 3/4 cup sugar and vanilla extract. Beat until thoroughly blended. Spread over cheesecake and bake at 350°F for 10 minutes. Chill 8 hours or overnight.

. . . .

creamy cheesecake

Crust:
1/4 cup butter, melted
1 cup graham cracker crumbs
1/4 cup sugar

Filling:

2 (8-ounce) packages cream cheese, softened
1 (14-ounce) can sweetened condensed milk
3 eggs
1/4 teaspoon salt
1/4 cup fresh lemon juice

Topping:

1 (8-ounce) carton sour cream

To prepare crust: Combine butter, crumbs, and sugar well; pat firmly into bottom of buttered 9- or 10-inch springform pan; set aside.

To prepare filling: Beat cream cheese until light and fluffy. Beat in condensed milk well. Add eggs one at a time, beating well after each addition. Add salt and beat until smooth. Stir in lemon juice. Pour over crust. Bake at 300°F for 50 to 55 minutes. Cool to room temperature; chill 8 hours or overnight.

For topping: Spread sour cream on cheesecake. Garnish as desired.

. . . .

cheesecakes supreme

Makes 3 cheesecake pies or 1 very large cheesecake

Crust:

3-3/4 cups graham cracker crumbs
3/4 cup sugar
3/4 cup butter

Filling:

5 (8-ounce) packages cream cheese, softened
1-3/4 cup sugar
3 tablespoons flour
1-1/2 teaspoons grated lemon zest
1-1/2 teaspoons grated orange zest

1 teaspoon grated lime zest
1/4 teaspoon vanilla extract
5 eggs
2 egg yolks
1/4 cup whipping cream

Topping:

Fresh strawberries and whipped cream (optional)

To prepare crust: Combine graham cracker crumbs, 3/4 cup sugar, and butter; stir well. Press mixture into three 9-inch pie plates or one large springform pan.

To prepare filling: Beat cream cheese until soft and creamy. Gradually add 1-3/4 cups sugar, beating until fluffy. Add flour, citrus zest, and vanilla extract. Mix well. Add whole eggs and egg yolks one at a time, beating well after each addition. Stir in whipping cream. Pour into prepared crusts; bake at 400°F for 5 minutes. Reduce heat to 250°F and bake 30 minutes or until set. Cool. Chill 8 hours or overnight. Cheesecakes may be covered securely with plastic wrap and frozen.

To prepare topping: Spread sweetened fresh strawberries over cheesecake and top with dollops of sweetened whipped cream, if desired.

· · · · · · · · · ·

chocolate cheesecake

Crust:

2 cups graham cracker crumbs
1/2 cup melted butter
1/4 cup sugar
1/8 teaspoon cinnamon

Filling:

16 ounces cream cheese, softened
1 cup sugar
4 eggs separated
2 (6-ounce) packages semi-sweet chocolate bits
1/2 cup hot strong coffee
1/8 teaspoon salt
1 teaspoon vanilla extract

Topping:

1 cup heavy whipping cream
4 tablespoons sugar

To prepare crust: Butter bottom and sides of a 9-inch springform pan. Blend graham cracker crumbs, butter, sugar, and cinnamon and pat mixture into bottom and up sides of pan; set aside.

To prepare filling: Preheat oven to 350°F. Beat cream cheese until fluffy. Add 1/3 cup sugar gradually; continue beating until well blended. Add egg yolks one at a time, beating well after each addition. Melt chocolate bits in a double boiler over hot, but not boiling, water. Blend in coffee, salt, and vanilla extract and blend all into the cream cheese mixture.

Beat egg whites to soft peaks; add remaining sugar until glossy peaks appear. Fold egg whites gently into chocolate mixture and pour into prepared crust. Bake at 350°F for 1 hour. Do not open oven door during baking. Turn oven off, but leave cake inside for 1 hour until completely cooled. Remove cake from oven; chill 8 hours or overnight.

To prepare topping: Whip cream and gradually add sugar. Spread over top of cake.

. . . .

gingersnap cheesecake

Crust:

2 cups finely ground gingersnap crumbs
1/4 cup sugar
1/4 pound butter, melted

Filling:

1 (8-ounce) package cream cheese, softened
1 (14-ounce) can sweetened condensed milk
1/3 cup fresh lime juice
1/3 cup ginger marmalade
1 cup sliced fresh fruit (peaches, pineapple, or nectarines are preferable)

To prepare crust: Combine gingersnap crumbs, sugar, and butter and blend thoroughly. Line the bottom and halfway up the sides of a 9-inch springform pan.

To prepare filling: Beat cream cheese until light and fluffy. Beat in condensed milk. Beat in lime juice. Add marmalade and stir until well blended.

Line crust with sliced fruit. Pour cheese mixture over fruit and refrigerate for 2 hours or until cake is set.

· · · · · · · · · ·

gingersnap cheesecake supreme

2 (3-ounce) packages cream cheese
24 chopped maraschino cherries
2 cups chopped pecans
1 cup whipping cream
3 tablespoons sugar
1 tablespoon unflavored gelatin
2-1/2 cups gingersnap crumbs
2 tablespoons cold water

Cream cheese until very soft. Blend in cherries and nuts. Whip cream until it begins to thicken and hold its shape. Beat in sugar and blend well. Stir in gelatin which has been softened in cold water and dissolved over hot water. Gradually fold into cream cheese mixture.

In a paper-lined pan, arrange alternate layers of gingersnap crumbs and cheese mixture. Chill approximately 12 hours before serving.

· · · · · · · · ·

lemon cheesecake

A very light and delicious cheesecake, especially good during the summer because no baking is necessary.

Crust:
1-1/2 cups graham cracker crumbs
3 tablespoons sugar
4 ounces butter

Filling:
1 (3-ounce) package lemon gelatin
1 cup water
1 (8-ounce) package cream cheese
1 cup sugar
1 teaspoon lemon flavoring
1 (13-ounce) evaporated milk, chilled and whipped
3/4 cup graham cracker crumbs

To prepare crust: Combine graham cracker crumbs, sugar, and butter well and press into square baking dish; set aside.
To prepare filling: Mix gelatin with 1 cup boiling water until completely dissolved; set aside to cool. Mix cream cheese, sugar, and flavoring until light and fluffy. Add cooled gelatin and milk; pour slowly over crust.

Sprinkle top evenly with graham cracker crumbs. Chill well before serving. Cut into squares to serve, if desired.

. . . .

chocolate marble cheesecake

Crust:
1 cup graham cracker crumbs
3 tablespoons sugar
3 tablespoons melted butter

Filling:
3 (8-ounce) packages cream cheese, softened
1 cup sugar
3 tablespoons flour
1 teaspoon vanilla extract
3 eggs
6 to 7 tablespoons milk
1 (1-ounce) square unsweetened chocolate, melted

To prepare crust: Combine graham cracker crumbs, sugar, and melted butter and press into bottom of 9-inch springform pan; set aside.

To prepare filling: Combine cream cheese, sugar, flour, and vanilla extract, mixing until well blended. Blend in eggs and milk, mixing well. Blend chocolate into 1 cup batter. Spoon plain and chocolate batters alternately over crust; draw a knife through batter several times to create a marble effect. Bake at 450°F for 10 minutes. Reduce oven temperature to 250°F and continue baking 30 minutes. Loosen cake from rim of pan. Spread top of cake with sweetened whipped cream, if desired. Chill before serving.

. . . .

white chocolate cheesecake

Crust:
1/4 pound butter, melted
2 cups very finely ground tea biscuit crumbs
1 ounce white chocolate, grated
1/4 cup sugar

Filling:
4 (8-ounce) packages cream cheese
1-1/4 cups sugar
Pinch of salt
4 large eggs
3 ounces white chocolate, shaved or
   sliced thin

Topping:
2 cups sour cream
1/4 cup sugar
1 teaspoon vanilla extract
1 ounce white chocolate, shaved thin

To prepare crust: Combine butter, tea biscuit crumbs, chocolate, and sugar until well blended. Press mixture over sides and bottom of an ungreased 10-inch springform pan.

To prepare filling: Preheat oven to 350°F. Combine cream cheese and sugar and beat until soft and fluffy. Add salt and mix well. With electric mixer on lowest speed, add eggs one at a time just until egg has been incorporated into batter. Add shaved white chocolate and fold in. Pour into crust. Bake at 350°F for 40 minutes. Remove cake from oven. Let stand for 10 minutes.

To prepare topping: Combine sour cream, sugar, and vanilla extract, spread over top of cake. Bake at 350°F for 10 minutes. Remove from oven and refrigerate immediately. When completely chilled, decorate top of cake with shaved white chocolate.

chocolate swirl cheesecake

Crust:
2 cups very finely ground vanilla or chocolate wafer crumbs
1/4 pound butter
1/4 cup sugar

Filling:
4 (8-ounce packages) cream cheese
1-1/4 cups sugar
1-1/2 teaspoons vanilla extract
Pinch of salt
4 large eggs
1-1/2 ounces German sweet chocolate, melted
1/2 teaspoon instant coffee powder

Topping:
2 cups sour cream
3/4 cup sugar
1 teaspoon vanilla extract

To prepare crust: Combine cookie crumbs, butter, and sugar until well blended. Press mixture over sides and bottom of ungreased 10-inch springform pan.

To prepare filling: Combine cream cheese and sugar; beat until soft and fluffy. Add vanilla extract and salt, blend thoroughly. Add eggs one at a time, keeping mixer at low speed to prevent too much air from being blended into the batter. Mix just until each egg is incorporated into the batter.

Preheat oven to 350°F. Reserve one cup of batter. Pour remaining batter over crust. Add melted chocolate and instant coffee powder to reserved cup of batter and blend well. Pour chocolate mixture into center of batter in the pan and draw a knife through the two batters in a swirling pattern. Keep most of the chocolate in the center. Bake at 350°F for 1 hour. Cool for 10 minutes while preparing topping. **To prepare topping:** Combine sour cream, sugar, and vanilla extract. Spread over top of cake and return to 350°F oven for 10 minutes. Remove cake from oven and cool. Refrigerate 8 hours or overnight.

. . . .

praline cheesecake

Crust:
1-1/2 cups graham cracker crumbs
1/4 cup sugar
1/4 cup chopped pecans, toasted
1/4 cup butter, melted

Filling:
3 (8-ounce) packages cream cheese, softened
1 cup firmly packed brown sugar
1 (5-1/3 ounce) can evaporated milk
2 tablespoons cake flour
1-1/2 teaspoons vanilla extract
3 eggs
1 cup pecan halves, toasted
1 cup dark corn syrup
1/4 cup cornstarch
2 tablespoons brown sugar
1 teaspoon vanilla extract

To prepare crust: Combine crumbs, sugar, and pecans. Stir in melted butter. Press mixture into bottom and 1-1/2 inches up sides of springform pan. Bake at 350°F for 8 to 10 minutes or until set.

To prepare filling: Beat cream cheese, 1 cup brown sugar, evaporated milk, flour, and 1-1/2 teaspoons vanilla extract until light and fluffy. Add eggs, beating just until blended. Pour mixture into baked crust. Bake at 350°F for 50 to 55 minutes, or until set. Cool in pan for 30 minutes, loosen sides, remove rim from pan. Cool completely. Arrange pecan halves over top.

Before serving, combine syrup, cornstarch, and 2 tablespoons brown sugar in small saucepan. Cook and stir until thick and bubbly. Remove from heat, stir in vanilla extract. Cool slightly. Serve cheesecake with warm sauce.

. . . .

perfect cheesecake

Crust:
1/2 cup graham cracker crumbs
1 tablespoon sugar
1/4 teaspoon cinnamon
1/4 teaspoon nutmeg
2 tablespoons butter, melted

Filling:
5 (8-ounce) packages cream cheese, softened
1-3/4 cups sugar
6 eggs
3 tablespoons plain flour
3/4 teaspoon salt
1/2 cup whipping cream
3/4 teaspoon grated lemon zest
1/4 teaspoon vanilla extract
3/4 teaspoon grated orange zest
1 (8-ounce) carton sour cream

To prepare crust: Blend crumbs, sugar, cinnamon, nutmeg, and butter; press mixture into bottom and up sides of a greased springform pan.
To prepare filling: Blend cream cheese until soft and fluffy. Add sugar gradually, beating well after each addition. Add eggs one at a time, continuing to beat well. Add sifted flour and salt alternately with whipping cream, blending thoroughly. Add vanilla extract and orange zest.

Bake at 325°F for 1 hour or until set. Top with sour cream and bake at 325°F for 5 minutes. Cool thoroughly before removing side of springform pan.

. . . .

strawberry white chocolate cheesecake

Crust:
1 cup graham cracker crumbs
3 tablespoons sugar
3 tablespoons butter, melted

Filling:
4 (8-ounce) packages cream cheese, softened
1 cup sugar
1 tablespoon vanilla extract
4 large eggs
1/4 cup sour cream
4 ounces white chocolate, melted
1/2 cup strawberry preserves
Fresh whole strawberries (optional)

To prepare crust: Combine crumbs, sugar, and butter and blend well. Press into bottom of a 9-inch springform pan; set aside.

To prepare filling: With an electric mixer, beat cream cheese until smooth. Gradually add sugar, beating until light and fluffy. Add vanilla extract and eggs, beating gently until well blened. Add sour cream and stir until blended. Fold chocolate into creamed mixture. Swirl in preserves to give a marble effect. Pour batter into prepared crust. Bake at 400°F for 10 minutes. Reduce heat to 275°F and bake 1 hour. Turn off oven and open door slightly. Allow cheesecake to completely cool in oven. Chill for 8 hours or overnight. Garnish with fresh whole strawberries, if desired.

. . . .

sweet potato cheesecake

Crust:
1-2/3 cups graham cracker crumbs
1/3 cup butter, melted
4 tablespoons sugar

Filling:
2 envelopes unflavored gelatin
1/2 cup cold water
3 eggs, separated
3/4 cup sugar
1/2 teaspoon salt
1/3 cup milk
2 (8-ounce) packages cream cheese, softened
1-1/4 cups cooked, mashed sweet potatoes
1 cup whipping cream, whipped
1/2 teaspoon vanilla extract

Topping:
1 cup whipping cream, whipped and sweetened to taste
Mandarin orange slices (optional)

To prepare crust: Combine crumbs, butter, and sugar and blend well. Press into a 9-inch springform pan and chill until set.

To prepare filling: Soften gelatin in cold water in top of a double boiler; stir in egg yolks, sugar, salt, and milk. Place over water and bring water to a boil. Reduce heat, then cook, stirring constantly, until slightly thickened. Beat cream cheese and sweet potatoes together until light and fluffy. Combine gelatin and cream cheese mixtures and blend until smooth. Beat egg whites until stiff but not dry. Fold egg whites, whipped cream, and vanilla extract into the batter. Spoon into prepared pan. Chill until set. Garnish with dollops of whipped cream and orange slices, if desired.

pumpkin cheesecake

Crust:
1-1/2 cups biscuit mix
2 tablespoons sugar
1/4 cup butter

Filling:
1 (8-ounce) package cream cheese,
    softened
3/4 cup sugar
3 eggs
6 to 7 tablespoons milk
2 tablespoons flour

1 teaspoon cinnamon
1/4 teaspoon ground ginger
1/4 teaspoon nutmeg
1 (16-ounce) can pumpkin
1/4 teaspoon vanilla extract

Topping:
1-1/2 cups sour cream
2 tablespoons sugar
1/4 teaspoon vanilla extract

To prepare crust: Combine biscuit mix and sugar, stirring well; cut in butter with a pastry blender or 2 knives until mixture resembles coarse meal. Press mixture into a 9-inch square baking pan.

To prepare filling: Beat cream cheese; gradually add sugar, beating until light and fluffy, until sugar dissolves. Add eggs one at a time, beating well after each addition. Add milk. Combine flour, cinnamon, ginger, and nutmeg; stir well. Add to creamed mixture, beating well. Add pumpkin and vanilla extract to creamed mixture, mixing well. Pour batter into crust. Bake at 350°F for 55 minutes or until set.

To prepare topping: Beat sour cream and add 2 tablespoons sugar and 1/4 teaspoon vanilla extract; beat until sugar is dissolved and well blended. Spread over cheesecake while cake is hot. Chill 6 hours or overnight.

. . . .

coffee
cakes

Even the crumbs are delicious.

apple coffee cake

1/4 cup butter
3/4 cup sugar
1 egg
1-3/4 cups cake flour
2 teaspoons baking powder
1/2 teaspoon nutmeg

1/4 teaspoon salt
2/3 cup milk
1 teaspoon vanilla extract
1 cup finely chopped cooking apples
1/3 cup sugar
1 teaspoon cinnamon

Cream butter; gradually add 3/4 cup sugar, beating well. Add egg, beating well.

Sift together flour, baking powder, nutmeg, and salt; add to creamed mixture alternately with milk, mixing well after each addition. Stir in vanilla extract. Pour batter into a greased and floured 9-inch square baking pan.

Combine apples, 1/3 cup sugar, and cinnamon; mix well. Sprinkle over batter. Bake at 350°F for 25 to 30 minutes or until tests done.

apricot orange coffee cake

1 (8-ounce) package dried apricots
1/2 cup chopped pecans
1/4 cup cake flour
1 cup sugar
2 tablespoons butter
1 egg

2 cups cake flour
2 teaspoons baking powder
1/4 teaspoon baking soda
1/4 teaspoon salt
1/2 cup orange juice
1/4 cup water

Soak apricots in warm water to cover for 30 minutes; drain well and cut into 1/4-inch pieces.

Combine apricot pieces and pecans; dredge with 1/4 cup flour; set aside.

Combine sugar and butter, beating until light and fluffy. Add egg and beat well. Sift 2 cups flour, baking powder, baking soda, and salt. Combine orange juice and water. Add flour and orange juice mixtures alternately to creamed ingredients, mixing lightly after each addition. Stir in apricots and pecans.

Spoon batter into wax paper-lined and greased 9 x 5 x 3-inch loaf pan. Bake at 350°F for 1 hour or until tests done.

apricot pecan coffee cake

1 (16-ounce) can apricot halves
1/3 cup vegetable shortening
1/2 cup sugar
2 eggs
2 cups cake flour

1/2 teaspoon salt
1 teaspoon baking powder
1/2 teaspoon baking soda
1/2 cup chopped pecans

Drain apricots, reserving syrup; press apricots through a sieve or food mill. Add enough reserved syrup to apricots to make 1 cup; set aside.

Cream shortening and sugar until fluffy. Add eggs one at a time, beating well after each addition.

Sift dry ingredients together and add alternately with apricots to creamed mixture; stir just until all ingredients are moistened. Stir in pecans. Spoon batter into a well-greased 9 x 5 x 3-inch loaf pan. Bake at 350°F for 50 minutes or until tests done.

banana coffee cake

1/2 cup butter
1 cup sugar
2 eggs
2 cups flour

1 teaspoon baking soda
Pinch of salt
1 cup chopped pecans
3 ripe bananas, mashed

Mix butter, sugar, and eggs together. Add dry ingredients, then bananas and nuts. Pour into a greased 9 x 5 x 3-inch loaf pan. Bake at 325°F for 40 to 50 minutes or until tests done.

banana date nut coffee cake

2 cups cake flour
1 teaspoon baking soda
1 teaspoon salt
1/2 cup vegetable shortening
1 cup sugar
2 whole eggs

1 teaspoon vanilla extract
2 or 3 small bananas, mashed
1/2 cup chopped pecans
1/2 cup chopped dates
1/4 cup flour

Sift flour, baking soda, and salt together; set aside. Cream shortening and sugar until light and fluffy. Add eggs one at a time, beating well after each addition. Blend in vanilla extract, then flour mixture alternately with the bananas. Dredge pecans and dates in 1/4 cup flour and fold into mixture. Pour into a greased and floured 9 x 5 x 3-inch loaf pan. Bake at 325°F for approximately 45 minutes. Serve plain or with cream cheese.

banana cranberry coffee cake

2 cups fresh cranberries
1 cup sugar
1 cup water
1/3 cup vegetable shortening
2/3 cup sugar
2 eggs

2 cups cake flour
2 teaspoons baking powder
1/2 teaspoon salt
1/4 teaspoon baking soda
1 cup mashed bananas
1/2 cup chopped pecans

Combine cranberries, 1 cup sugar, and water; cook over medium heat approximately 5 minutes or until cranberries begin to pop. Drain; set aside.

Cream shortening; gradually add 2/3 cup sugar, beating until light and fluffy. Add eggs one at a time, beating well after each addition. Sift flour, baking powder, salt, and baking soda; add to creamed mixture alternately with banana, mixing well after each addition. Fold in cranberries and pecans.

Line a greased 9 x 5 x 3-inch loaf pan with wax paper; grease wax paper. Spoon batter into pan. Bake at 350°F for 1 hour or until tests done. Cool 5 or 10 minutes in pan and then remove.

. . . .

chocolate coconut coffee cake

1 tablespoon lemon juice	1 cup sugar
2-1/2 cups unsifted flour	1 egg
1-1/2 teaspoons baking soda	6 ounces cocoa
1-1/2 teaspoons salt	1 teaspoon vanilla extract
4 tablespoons butter	1-1/4 cups milk
3 ounces cream cheese	1 cup flaked coconut, toasted

Combine milk with lemon juice; set aside. Combine flour, baking soda, and salt; set aside.

Cream butter and cream cheese and gradually add sugar, beating well. Beat in egg and then add cocoa and vanilla extract, blending well.

To this mixture, alternately blend in milk and flour mixtures. Stir in coconut.

Pour batter into a well-greased 9 x 5 x 3-inch loaf pan. Bake at 350°F for 1 hour, or until tests done. Allow to cool for 5 to 10 minutes in pan; remove to cake plate. Cool completely before slicing.

. . . .

banana sour cream coffee cake

1/2 cup chopped pecans	1 teaspoon baking soda
1/4 cup sugar	1/2 cup sour cream
1/4 teaspoon cinnamon	1 teaspoon vanilla extract
1/2 cup vegetable shortening	1 cup mashed bananas
1 cup sugar	1 teaspoon baking powder
2 eggs	1/4 teaspoon salt
2-1/2 cups cake flour	

Combine pecans, 1/4 cup sugar, and cinnamon, stir well; set aside. Cream shortening and 1 cup sugar until light and fluffy. Add eggs one at a time, beating well after each addition. Add flour alternately with sour cream; stir in the vanilla extract and bananas just enough to blend.

Sprinkle half of reserved cinnamon mixture into bottom of a well-greased bundt pan; spoon half of batter into pan. Sprinkle remaining cinnamon mixture over batter, then spoon remaining batter into pan. Bake at 350°F for 40 to 45 minutes or until tests done.

Cool cake 5 minutes in pan on a wire rack. Serve warm or cold.

. . . .

carrot pecan coffee cake

1-3/4 cups cake flour
1 teaspoon cinnamon
1 teaspoon baking soda
1/2 teaspoon salt
3/4 cup salad oil
1 cup sugar
2 eggs
1 cup grated carrots
1 cup chopped pecans

Combine flour, cinnamon, baking soda, and salt; set aside.

Combine oil, sugar, and eggs, beating until well blended. Add dry ingredients and mix just until blended. Fold in carrots and pecans and spoon batter into a greased and floured 9 x 5 x 3-inch loaf pan. Bake at 350°F for 1 hour and 25 minutes or until tests done. Cool in pan for 10 minutes and remove from pan to cool completely.

. . . .

cinnamon buttermilk coffee cake

2-1/2 cups cake flour
1/2 cups firmly packed brown sugar
1/2 cup butter
1/3 cup cake flour
1 egg

1 cup buttermilk
1 teaspoon baking soda
1 teaspoon cinnamon
2 cups chopped pecans

Combine 2-1/2 cups flour and sugar in a large mixing bowl. Cut in butter until mixture resembles coarse meal. Set aside 3/4 cup crumb mixture.

Combine remaining crumb mixture and 1/3 cup flour. Add egg, buttermilk, baking soda, and cinnamon; stir until moistened.

Pour batter into a greased 9-inch square pan. Combine reserved crumb mixture with nuts; sprinkle over batter. Bake at 325°F for 1 hour or until tests done. Cut into squares.

. . . .

cranberry coffee cake

1/2 cup butter
1 cup sugar
2 eggs
2-1/2 cups cake flour
1 teaspoon baking powder
1 teaspoon baking soda

1 (8-ounce) carton sour cream
1 teaspoon vanilla extract
1 (16-ounce) can whole berry cranberry sauce
1/2 cup chopped pecans

Cream butter and gradually add sugar, beating until light and creamy. Add eggs one at a time, beating well after each addition. Combine flour, baking powder, and baking soda and add alternately with sour cream, beating well. Blend in vanilla extract.

Spoon 1/3 of the mixture into a greased and floured 10-inch bundt or tube pan. Spread 1/3 cranberry sauce over batter. Repeat layers twice more, ending with cranberry sauce. Sprinkle pecans over top.

Bake at 325°F for 1 hour or until done. Let cool 5 minutes before removing from pan. Drizzle **Glaze** over top.

glaze

1 cup confectioners sugar
1/2 teaspoon vanilla extract
2 tablespoons milk

Combine all ingredients; stir well and drizzle over warm cake.

. . . .

cherry chocolate coffee cake

1 square unsweetened chocolate
2 tablespoons water
1/2 cup vegetable shortening
1 cup sugar
1-1/2 cups cake flour
1 teaspoon baking soda

1/2 teaspoon salt
2/3 cup buttermilk mixed with 2 tablespoons cherry juice
1 egg
1/4 cup well-drained maraschino cherries, cut in eighths

Preheat oven to 350°F. Grease an 8 x 8 x 2-inch pan, line bottom with wax paper, grease paper; set aside.

Put chocolate and water into a custard cup and set in hot water to melt. Stir until smooth and cool.

Cream shortening, add sugar and beat until light and fluffy. Sift flour with baking soda and salt 3 times. Add alternately with buttermilk and cherry juice, beating well after each addition. Add egg and cooled chocolate and beat in well.

Pour batter into prepared pan. Sprinkle cherries over top of batter. Bake approximately 35 minutes. Cool in pan on wire rack 5 minutes, then turn out onto rack and strip off paper. When cool, spread top with **Coffee Butter Frosting.**

coffee butter frosting

1/4 cup butter, softened
2 cups sifted confectioners sugar
3 tablespoons hot brewed coffee
1/4 teaspoon salt
1 tablespoon light corn syrup

Cream butter until smooth and shiny; gradually blend in sugar alternately with approximately 3 tablespoons coffee. Beat in salt and white corn syrup until mixture is spreadable. Very good for chocolate, white, and yellow cakes.

. . . .

strawberry pecan coffee cake

3-1/2 cups cake flour
1 teaspoon salt
2 cups sugar
1 tablespoon cinnamon
1 teaspoon baking soda

4 eggs
1-1/4 cups vegetable oil
2 cups thawed sliced frozen strawberries
1-1/4 cups chopped pecans

Combine flour, salt, sugar, cinnamon, and baking soda. Add eggs, oil, strawberries, and pecans; stir just until all ingredients are moistened.

Spoon batter into two well-greased 9 x 5 x 3-inch loaf pans. Bake at 350°F for 1 hour to 1 hour and 10 minutes or until tests done. Cool in pan for 5 minutes; remove to wire rack to cool.

. . . .

fig coffee cake

1/2 cup firmly packed brown sugar
2 tablespoons butter, softened
1/2 teaspoon cinnamon
10 fig-filled bar cookies, crumbled
2 eggs
3/4 cup sugar

1/3 cup butter, melted
2 cups cake flour
1 teaspoon baking powder
1/2 teaspoon salt
1 teaspoon vanilla extract
1/2 cup milk

Combine brown sugar, softened butter, cinnamon, and cookies, mixing well; set aside.

Beat eggs until frothy; add sugar and melted butter and beat well. Sift flour, baking powder, and salt and add alternately with milk, mixing well. Stir in vanilla extract.

Pour half of batter into a greased and floured 8-inch square pan; top with half of cookie mixture. Pour remainder of batter over cookie layer. Sprinkle remaining cookie mixture on top. Bake at 350°F for 40 to 45 minutes or until cake tests done.

honey coffee cake

1 cup all-purpose flour
1 cup whole wheat flour
1-1/2 teaspoons baking powder
1 teaspoon baking soda
1 teaspoon salt
1/2 teaspoon cinnamon

1/2 teaspoon ground ginger
1 large egg
1 cup milk
1/2 cup honey
1/4 cup vegetable oil
1/2 cup pecans, chopped

Line bottom of 9 x 5 x 3-inch loaf pan with wax paper; grease paper. Combine flours, baking powder, baking soda, salt, cinnamon, and ginger; set aside.

Beat egg until foamy; add milk, honey, and oil; beat to blend. Add flour mixture and stir until moistened. Stir in pecans. Turn into prepared pan. Bake at 350°F for 45 to 50 minutes or until tests done. Cool 5 minutes in pan and then turn out onto a wire rack. Remove wax paper; turn right side up. Cool completely before serving.

lemon coffee cake no. 1

1/2 cup butter
1 cup sugar
2 eggs
2 cups cake flour
1 teaspoon baking powder

1/2 teaspoon salt
1/2 cup milk
1/2 cup chopped pecans
Grated zest of 1 lemon

Cream butter and sugar until light and fluffy. Add eggs one at a time, beating well after each addition. Sift flour, baking powder, and salt together, and add alternately with milk, mixing well after each addition. Stir in pecans and lemon zest.

Pour batter into a greased and floured 9 x 5 x 3-inch pan. Bake at 350°F for 55 minutes or until tests done. Pour **Lemon Glaze** over cake. Cool 10 to 15 minutes before removing from pan.

lemon glaze

1/2 cup confectioners sugar
Juice of 1 lemon

Combine ingredients, mixing well. Pour over warm cake.

. . . .

lemon coffee cake no. 2

3/4 cup butter
1-1/2 cups granulated sugar
3 eggs
2-1/2 cups cake flour
1/4 teaspoon baking soda
1/4 teaspoon salt

1/2 cup buttermilk
3/4 cup chopped pecans
Grated zest of 1 lemon
Juice of 2 lemons
3/4 cup confectioners sugar

Cream butter and granulated sugar until light and fluffy. Add eggs one at a time, beating well after each addition. Sift flour, baking soda, and salt together and add alternately with buttermilk; stir just until all ingredients are moistened. Stir in pecans and lemon zest. Spoon batter into a greased and floured 9 x 5 x 3-inch loaf pan. Bake at 325°F for 1 hour and 15 minutes, or until tests done.

Cool for 15 minutes and remove from pan.

Combine lemon juice and granulated sugar; stir well. Punch holes in top of warm cake and pour lemon juice mixture onto cake.

pecan sugar coffee cake

2/3 cup butter	1 teaspoon baking soda
1 cup sugar	1/2 teaspoon salt
1/2 cup firmly packed brown sugar	1 teaspoon cinnamon
2 eggs	1 cup buttermilk
1 teaspoon vanilla extract	1 cup chopped pecans
2-1/2 cups cake flour	1/2 cup brown sugar, firmly packed
1 teaspoon baking powder	1/2 teaspoon cinnamon

Cream butter and 1 cup sugar and 1/2 cup brown sugar until light and fluffy. Add eggs one at a time, beating well after each addition; stir in vanilla extract.

Sift flour, baking powder, baking soda, salt, and 1 teaspoon cinnamon together. Add alternately with buttermilk, mixing well after each addition.

Pour batter into a greased and floured 9 x 5 x 3-inch loaf pan. Combine pecans, 1/2 cup brown sugar, and 1/2 teaspoon cinnamon; stir well and sprinkle over batter.

Bake at 350°F for 35 minutes or until tests done.

sour cream coffee cake

Cake:

1/2 cup pecans, chopped	2 teaspoons cinnamon
2 tablespoons brown sugar, firmly packed	1 cup butter
	1 cup sugar

2 eggs
2-1/2 cups cake flour
1 teaspoon baking soda
1 teaspoon baking powder
1 cup sour cream

Glaze:
1-1/4 cups confectioners sugar, sifted
1 tablespoon milk
1/4 teaspoon vanilla extract

To prepare cake: Combine pecans, brown sugar, and cinnamon, stir well; set aside.
Cream butter and sugar, beating until fluffy. Add eggs one at a time and beat
well. Sift flour, baking soda, and baking powder together and add alternately with
sour cream. Spoon half into a greased and floured bundt pan; sprinkle half of pecan
mixture over batter. Repeat layers. Bake at 350°F for 35 to 40 minutes. Cool 5 minutes and turn onto serving plate. Store overnight in airtight container, after driz-
zling glaze over top.
To prepare glaze: Combine all ingredients and stir until smooth. Drizzle over cake.

. . . .

sour cream coffee cake supreme

3 cups cake flour
1-1/2 teaspoons baking powder
1-1/2 teaspoons baking soda
1/4 teaspoon salt
3 sticks butter, at room temperature
1-1/2 cups sugar
3 large eggs
1-1/2 cups sour cream

1-1/2 teaspoons vanilla extract
1 cup brown sugar, firmly packed
1 cup walnuts or pecans, chopped
1-1/2 teaspoons cinnamon
2 tablespoons vanilla extract
2 tablespoons milk
Confectioners sugar

Butter a 10-inch tube pan. Sift flour, baking powder, baking soda, and salt together. Combine butter and sugar and beat until soft and fluffy. Add eggs one at a time, beating well after each addition. Blend in sour cream and vanilla extract alternately with sifted dry ingredients, beating well.

Combine brown sugar, nuts, and cinnamon.

Put a 1/3 of the batter into the tube pan. Sprinkle 1/2 of the brown sugar mixture over it. Repeat with a 1/3 of the batter and remaining brown sugar mixture. Top with remaining 1/3 of batter.

Combine vanilla extract and milk and spoon over the top. Bake at 325°F for 1 hour to 1 hour and 10 minutes. Cool 10 minutes before removing from pan. Dust generously with confectioners sugar.

lemon light coffee cake

3/4 cup evaporated milk
2 tablespoons vinegar
1 teaspoon baking soda
1/2 cup butter, softened
1 cup sugar
2 eggs
1 teaspoon grated lemon zest

1-3/4 cups cake flour
2 teaspoons baking powder
1/2 teaspoon salt
1/2 cup brown sugar, firmly packed
1 tablespoon cinnamon
1 cup sifted confectioners sugar
2 tablespoons lemon juice

Combine evaporated milk and vinegar, stir in baking soda; set aside.

Cream butter and sugar until light and fluffy. Add eggs one at a time, beating well after each addition. Add lemon zest; beat well.

Sift flour, baking powder, and salt together; add to creamed mixture alternately with milk and vinegar, beating well after each addition. Spread 1/2 of the batter in a greased and floured 10-inch tube pan.

Combine brown sugar and cinnamon; sprinkle 1/2 of the mixture over batter. Spoon remaining batter into pan; sprinkle with remaining cinnamon and sugar. Bake at 350°F for approximately 45 minutes or until tests done. Cool in pan 5 minutes before removing cake to cool completely.

Combine confectioners sugar and lemon juice; spoon over warm cake.

orange pecan coffee cake

1/2 cup butter, softened
3/4 cup sugar
2 eggs
2 teaspoons grated orange zest
2-1/2 cups cake flour
2-1/2 teaspoons baking powder

1 teaspoon salt
3/4 cup orange juice
2-1/2 teaspoons orange juice
1/2 cup pecans, chopped
1/2 cup sifted confectioners sugar

Cream butter and 3/4 cup sugar until light and fluffy. Add eggs one at a time, beating well after each addition. Add grated orange zest, blending well.

Sift flour, baking powder, and salt. Add alternately with 3/4 cup orange juice, mixing well after each addition. Stir in pecans.

Pour batter into a greased 9 x 5 x 3-inch loaf pan. Bake at 350°F for 50 to 55 minutes or until tests done. Cool for 10 minutes in pan, then remove and cool completely.

Combine 2-1/2 teaspoons orange juice and confectioners sugar; drizzle over loaf. Wrap in plastic and store overnight before serving.

special strawberry jam coffee cake

3 cups cake flour
1 teaspoon salt
3/4 teaspoon cream of tartar
1-1/2 teaspoon baking soda
1-1/2 cups sugar
1 cup butter

1 teaspoon vanilla extract
1/4 teaspoon lemon juice
4 eggs
1 cup strawberry jam
1/2 cup buttermilk
1 cup chopped pecan or walnuts

Combine flour, salt, cream of tartar, and baking soda; set aside.

Combine sugar, butter, vanilla extract, and lemon juice and cream until light and fluffy. Add eggs one at a time, beating well after each addition. Combine jam and buttermilk; add to creamed mixture alternately with dry ingredients. mixing just until blended. Stir in nuts.

Spoon batter into two greased 9 x 5 x 3-inch loaf pans. Bake at 350°F for 55 minutes or until tests done. Cool 15 minutes; remove from pans onto wire racks. Serve plain or topped with sweetened whipped cream.

· · · · · · · · ·

spicy coffee cake

2-1/2 cups cake flour	1/2 cup pitted dates, cut fine
1 teaspoon baking soda	3 large eggs
1/2 teaspoon salt	1-3/4 cups sugar
1/2 teaspoon cinnamon	1 cup sour cream
1/2 teaspoon nutmeg	1/2 cup chopped pecans

Sift flour, baking soda, salt, cinnamon, and nutmeg together. Dredge dates in 1/2 cup of flour mixture; set aside. Beat eggs slightly; gradually beat in sugar until thickened; add sour cream and beat to blend. Gradually and gently beat in flour mixture until batter is smooth. Add pecans to date mixture and gently fold into batter.

Pour into a greased 9 x 9 x 1-3/4-inch cake pan. Bake at 350°F for approximately 35 to 40 minutes. Center may sink slightly but this will not affect texture. Loosen edges and turn onto a wire rack, then turn right side up and cool completely.

· · · · · · · · ·

strawberry coffee cake

2 cups cake flour	1/2 cup corn oil
1 teaspoon baking soda	10 ounces frozen sweetened
1/4 teaspoon salt	strawberries, thawed but
1 cup sugar	undrained; or 1 pint fresh
1/2 cup chopped pecans	sweetened strawberries
2 large eggs	

Grease and flour a 9 x 5 x 3-inch loaf pan. Sift flour, baking soda, and salt together; stir in sugar and pecans.

Beat eggs and oil until well blended; add undrained strawberries and beat just until blended. Add flour mixture and beat until mixture is smooth and strawberries are well distributed. Pour into prepared pan.

Bake at 350°F for 1 hour or until tests done. Cool before loosening edges and removing from pan. Cool completely.

. . . .

sweet potato coffee cake

1-1/2 cups sugar	1 teaspoon baking soda
1/2 cup vegetable oil	1 teaspoon nutmeg
2 eggs	1/2 teaspoon salt
1/3 cup milk	1 cup cooked sweet potatoes,
2 cups cake flour	mashed
1-1/2 teaspoons cinnamon	1 cup chopped pecans

Combine sugar, oil, eggs, and milk with an electric mixer; beat at medium speed just until combined.

Sift flour, cinnamon, baking soda, nutmeg, and salt together and add to egg mixture, mixing just until moistened. Stir in sweet potatoes and pecans.

Spoon batter into two greased and floured 9 x 5 x 3-inch loaf pans or 1-pound coffee cans. Bake at 350°F for 1 hour or until tests done. Let cool in pans or cans for 10 minutes; remove and complete cooling.

. . . .

tropical coffee cake

1/2 cup vegetable oil
1 cup sugar
2 eggs
2 cups cake flour
2 teaspoons baking powder
1/2 teaspoon salt
1 (8-ounce) carton peach-flavored yogurt
1 cup grated coconut
1/3 cup sugar
1 teaspoon cinnamon

Combine oil and 1 cup sugar and beat well. Add eggs one at a time, beating well after each addition. Add sifted flour, baking powder, and salt alternately with yogurt, blending well. Pour into a greased and floured 9-inch square pan.

Combine coconut, 1/3 cup sugar, and cinnamon. Sprinkle over top. Bake at 350°F for 40 minutes or until tests done.

. . . .

fruit
cakes

Experiment with these time-tested **favorites** to make *your own* famous cake.

chinese fruitcake

1 pound coconut
1 pound chopped pecans
1 pound dates, cut in small pieces

1/2 pound candied green cherries
1/2 pound candied red cherries
2 cans sweetened condensed milk

Grease large loaf pan or 2 small loaf pans. Combine all ingredients, blending well. Bake at 300°F for approximately 1 hour until top is brown.

. . . .

japanese fruit cake

1-2-2/3 cups sugar
1/3 cups butter
4-1/2 cups cake flour
5 eggs

1-1/2 teaspoons vanilla extract
1-1/3 cups milk
2-2/3 teaspoons baking powder

Cream butter and sugar together until light and fluffy. Add eggs one at a time, beating well after each addition. Add vanilla and divide batter into two parts. Sift dry ingredients together and add gradually to batter. To one part add:

1/4 cup chopped raisins
1/4 cup chopped pecans
1 teaspoon allspice
1/2 teaspoon cloves

Dredge raisins and pecans in flour.

Bake four 8-inch layers at 350°F for 20 to 25 minutes or until tests done. Bake cakes in two batches for best results. Spread with **Coconut Filling** and frost with **Seven-Minute Frosting**.

coconut filling

Juice and finely grated zest of 2
lemons
Meat of 1 large coconut, grated
2 cups sugar

1 cup boiling water
2 tablespoons cornstarch
1/2 cup cold water

Combine all ingredients, except cornstarch, in saucepan; mix well and place over medium heat. When mixture begins to boil, add cornstarch dissolved in water. Cook mixture until it turns clear and forms a thread when dropped from a spoon.

seven-minute frosting

2 egg whites
1-1/2 cups sugar
1/3 cup cold water

1-1/2 teaspoons light corn syrup
Pinch of salt
1 teaspoon vanilla extract

Combine ingredients in top of double boiler. Using an electric mixer, beat constantly over boiling water for seven minutes. Add vanilla extract. Frost entire cake.

fruit cake (small)

1 cup flour
1/4 teaspoon cinnamon
1/4 teaspoon ground cloves
1/4 teaspoon allspice
1/2 teaspoon baking powder
1/4 teaspoon mace
1/2 cup butter
1/2 cup brown sugar, packed
3 eggs

1 cup raisins
1 cup chopped figs
1 cup pecans, chopped
1/2 cup candied orange peel
1/2 cup candied lemon peel
1/4 cup maraschino cherries,
chopped
1/4 cup maraschino cherry juice

Sift all dry ingredients well except sugar. Cream butter and sugar until light and fluffy. Add eggs one at a time, beating well after each addition. Mix dry ingredients and fruit together; add cherry juice. Add fruit mixture to creamed mixture. Mix well. Pour into greased 8 x 5 x 3-inch pan. Bake at 250°F for approximately 2-1/2 hours.

southern frozen fruit cake

2 cups milk
1/4 cup cake flour
1/2 cup sugar
1/4 teaspoon salt
2 eggs
1 teaspoon vanilla extract

1 cup golden raisins
2 cups vanilla wafer crumbs
1/2 cup candied red cherries
1/4 cup candied green cherries
1 cup chopped pecans
1 cup whipping cream, whipped

Whip chilled whipping cream; set aside.

Scald milk in top of double boiler. Mix flour, sugar, and salt together; add to milk all at once and cook over hot water until smooth and thick. Stir constantly.

Pour mixture over beaten eggs gradually and return to double boiler, cooking approximately 3 minutes until thickened, stirring constantly. Add vanilla extract. Cool. Stir in raisins, crumbs, fruits, and nuts. (Reserve a few of the whole green and red fruits and pecans for garnish.) Fold in whipped cream.

Grease a 1-1/2-quart loaf pan and line the bottom with wax paper. Pour batter into pan. Arrange whole fruits and nuts over top of batter. Bake at 300°F for 1-1/2 hours. Wrap and freeze. Keeps approximately 2 weeks.

southern moist fruit cake

1 cup butter
2 cups sugar
6 eggs
3-1/2 cups cake flour
2 teaspoons baking soda
1/2 teaspoon salt
2 teaspoons cinnamon
1 teaspoon ground cloves
1 teaspoon nutmeg
1-1/2 pounds crystallized cherries
    (red and green)

1 cup dates
1-1/4 cup dark seedless raisins
1-1/4 cup light seedless raisins
2 cups cooked dried apples
1 cup chopped pecans
1 cup crushed pineapple, well
    drained
3/4 cup milk

Cream butter and sugar until light and fluffy. Add eggs one at a time, beating well after each addition. Sift flour, baking soda, salt, cinnamon, cloves, and nutmeg together. Cut fruits into small pieces. Dredge fruit well in 1 cup of flour mixture. Add fruit and remaining flour alternately with milk to batter.

Add pineapple and cooked apples to batter with your hands, mixing thoroughly.

Pour into greased and floured pans. Recipe yields batter for six (7-1/2 x 3-1/2 x 2-1/2-inches) loaf pans or 2 tube pans. Bake at 300°F. Bake loaf pans approximately 1 hour and tube pans approximately 1-1/2 hours or until tests done.

. . . .

southern lemon fruit cake

1 pound butter
1 pound light brown sugar
6 eggs, separated
3 teaspoons lemon juice
4 cups cake flour

1 teaspoon baking powder
1/2 pound candied cherries
1/2 pound candied pineapple
1 quart pecans

Cream butter and sugar. Add egg yolks one at a time, beating well after each addition. Add lemon juice and mix well. Sift 2 cups flour and baking powder together and stir into butter and sugar mixture. Cut pineapple, cherries, and nuts into small pieces, stir into 2 cups flour and mix into batter.

Beat egg whites until stiff peaks form; fold into cake mixture. Cover and let stand overnight in refrigerator. Stir well and pour into a greased tube pan lined with wax paper. Bake at 250°F for 3 hours or until tests done.

texas fruit cakes

- 1 pound pitted dates
- 1 pound pecans
- 1/2 pound candied cherries
- 1/2 pound candied pineapple
- 4 (3-1/2-ounce) cans flaked coconut
- 2 (14-ounce) cans sweetened condensed milk

Chop dates, nuts, and fruit. Combine all ingredients and mix well. Cover and let stand overnight in refrigerator.

Pour into miniature muffin tins. Bake at 325°F for 28 to 30 minutes or until golden brown. Do not overbake as the cakes tend to harden a bit after cooking. Will keep in an air-tight container for weeks.

white fruit cake southern style

- 2 cups sugar
- 1-1/2 cups butter
- 6 eggs
- 1/2 cup bourbon
- 1 teaspoon nutmeg
- 1 teaspoon vanilla extract
- 4 cups cake flour
- 2 teaspoons baking powder
- 1 pound candied cherries
- 1 pound candied pineapple, cut into large pieces
- 1 pound chopped pecans

Cream butter and sugar until light and fluffy. Add eggs one at a time, beating well after each addition. Add nutmeg, vanilla extract, and bourbon. Sift baking powder and 3 cups flour together and fold into the batter.

Dredge fruit in 1 cup flour and place fruit in the oven at 275°F for 5 minutes. Add flour-coated fruit to batter. Pour into tube pan. Bake 275°F for 3 hours.

fruit cake (unbaked)

2 cups raisins
1 cup dates
1 cup dried figs
1 cup candied lemon peel
1 cup candied orange peel
1 cup walnuts
1 cup pecans
1 pound graham crackers

1 cup butter
1 cup honey
2 teaspoons vanilla extract
2 teaspoons cinnamon
1 teaspoon mace
1/2 teaspoon nutmeg
1/2 teaspoon allspice

Cut up fruits and nuts. Roll graham crackers very fine or buy crackers already prepared. Cream butter and honey, add vanilla extract and let stand 2 hours. Add spices to cracker crumbs and combine with fruit and nut mixture.

Pack into loaf pans lined with wax paper. Store covered in a cool place.

perfect fruit cake

4 cups chopped pecans
2 cups crystallized cherries
5 slices crystallized pineapple, each slice cut into eighths
1 cup flour
1-1/2 teaspoons baking powder
1/4 teaspoon salt
4 eggs
1 cup sugar
1 teaspoon vanilla extract

Grease bottom and sides of a 2-quart tube pan and line bottom with brown paper or parchment paper.

Combine cherries and pineapple in a mixing bowl. Combine flour, baking powder, and salt and sift over the fruits.

Combine eggs, sugar, and vanilla extract in another mixing bowl and beat until blended. Pour over fruit and stir with a slotted spoon.

Pour batter into prepared pan. Bake at 250°F for 1-1/2 hours. Set cake pan into a pan of boiling water and continue baking 15 minutes longer.

pound
cakes

Make these cakes your cakes...

put some OOMPH !

into them!

almond pound cake

2/3 cup butter
1 cup sugar
3 eggs
1/2 cup blanched almonds, finely
ground

1/2 teaspoon almond flavoring
1-1/2 cups cake flour
1 teaspoon baking powder
1/4 cup blanched almonds, coarsely
chopped

Cream butter and add sugar gradually. Add eggs one at a time, beating well after each addition until light and fluffy. Add almonds and flavoring and mix thoroughly. Sift flour and baking powder together and add to batter; blend thoroughly.

Spoon into greased and floured 9 x 5 x 3-inch loaf pan and sprinkle with chopped almonds. Bake at 325°F for 45 to 50 minutes or until tests done.

apricot pound cake

1 cup butter
2-1/2 cups sugar
6 eggs
1 teaspoon orange extract
1 teaspoon rum extract
1 teaspoon vanilla extract

1/2 teaspoon lemon extract
3 cups flour
1/4 teaspoon baking powder
1/4 teaspoon salt
1 cup sour cream
1/2 cup apricot nectar

Cream together butter and sugar until light and fluffy. Add eggs one at a time, blending well after each addition. Stir in extracts well. Add sifted dry ingredients alternately with sour cream and apricot nectar.

Pour into a lightly greased 3-quart bundt or tube pan. Bake at 325°F for 1 hour and 15 minutes or until tests done.

buttermilk pound cake

1/2 cup vegetable shortening
2 sticks butter
3 cups sugar
5 large eggs
3 cups flour

1/2 teaspoon baking powder
3/4 cup buttermilk
1 teaspoon vanilla extract
1/4 teaspoon almond extract

Grease tube pan well with shortening; set aside. Cream butter and sugar together until light and fluffy. Add eggs one at a time, beating well after each addition. Sift flour and baking powder together and add alternately with buttermilk and vanilla and almond extracts. Bake, starting in cold oven, on middle rack, at 350°F for 1 hour and 20 minutes. The cake is best if cut the next day.

best pound cake

1-1/2 cups butter
2-1/4 cups sugar
8 large eggs, separated
2 teaspoons vanilla extract
2 tablespoons freshly squeezed
   lemon juice

3 cups cake flour
1/2 teaspoon mace
1/4 teaspoon baking soda
1/4 teaspoon salt
3/4 teaspoon cream of tartar
Confectioners sugar

Grease and flour a 3-1/2-quart bundt pan or a 10-inch tube pan; set aside. Cream butter until light and fluffy. Add sugar gradually, beating thoroughly. Beat in egg yolks one at a time, beating well after each addition. Stir in vanilla extract and lemon juice and blend well. Sift flour, mace, baking soda, and salt 3 times, then add to batter 1/2 cup at a time, beating well after each addition. Beat at least 10 minutes.

Beat egg whites and cream of tartar until soft peaks form; fold into creamed mixture. Bake at 300°F for 2 hours or until tests done. Turn off heat and leave in oven 30 minutes. Remove from oven and cool in pan on wire rack for 30 minutes. When completely cool, sprinkle with confectioners sugar.

banana pound cake

1 (16-ounce) box light brown sugar
1 cup granulated sugar
5 eggs
2 large bananas, mashed
3 cups flour
1/2 teaspoon baking powder

1/2 teaspoon salt
1/2 pound butter
1 cup milk
1 teaspoon vanilla extract
1 cup chopped pecans

Cream sugars with butter until light and fluffy. Add eggs one at a time, beating well after each addition. Stir in bananas.

Sift flour, baking powder, and salt together. Add to first mixture alternately with milk and vanilla extract. Stir in pecans. Pour into a well-greased tube. Bake at 325°F for 1-1/2 hours or until tests done.

Place upside down on a wire rack. When cooled, turn out onto rack.

. . . .

banana chocolate chip pound cake

1-1/2 cups butter, softened
3 cups sugar
6 large eggs, separated
1 tablespoon vanilla extract
3 cups cake flour
1/2 teaspoon baking powder

1/2 teaspoon baking soda
1 (8-ounce) carton sour cream
2 ripe bananas, mashed
1 (6-ounce) package semi-sweet
　　chocolate chips

Using an electric mixer, cream butter and sugar together until light and fluffy, approximately 10 minutes. Add egg yolks one at a time, beating well after each addition. Stir in vanilla extract. Sift flour, baking powder, and soda together 3 times. Add to creamed mixture alternately with sour cream, beginning and ending with flour mixture. Beat egg whites until stiff but not dry. Gently fold into batter. Fold in bananas. Dredge chocolate chips in a small amount of flour, then fold them into batter. Pour batter into a greased and floured 10-inch tube pan or two loaf pans. Bake at 325°F for approximately 1 hour and 15 minutes or until tests done. Cool in pan on a wire rack for approximately 10 minutes. Remove gently to complete cooling process.

. . . .

black walnut pound cake

1-1/2 cups butter, softened	3 cups cake flour
3 cups sugar	1 teaspoon baking powder
6 large eggs	1 cup whole milk
1 tablespoon vanilla extract	1 cup finely chopped black walnuts

Using an electric mixer, cream butter and sugar together until light and fluffy. Add eggs one at a time, beating well after each addition. Stir in vanilla extract. Sift flour and baking powder together. Add alternately with milk, beginning and ending with flour mixture. Dredge walnuts in a small amount of flour and fold in walnuts thoroughly. Pour into a greased and floured 10-inch tube pan. Bake at 300°F for approximately 1 hour and 15 minutes or until tests done. Cool in pan on a wire rack for approximately 10 minutes. Remove from pan to complete cooling process.

. . . .

brown sugar pound cake

1 cup butter, softened	3-1/2 cups cake flour
1/2 cup vegetable shortening	1/2 teaspoon baking powder
1 cup granulated sugar	1 cup milk
5 large eggs	2 cups chopped pecans
1 (16-ounce) package brown sugar, packed	2 tablespoons vanilla extract

Cream butter and shortening; gradually add sugar, beating until light and fluffy. Add eggs one at a time, beating well after each addition.

Combine flour and baking powder and sift 3 times. Add to creamed mixture alternately with milk, beginning and ending with flour mixture, and beating well after each addition.

Stir in pecans and vanilla extract.

Pour batter into a greased and floured 10-inch tube pan. Bake at 350°F for 1 hour and 10 minutes or until tests done. Cool in pan 10 minutes; invert onto wire rack and cool completely. Frost with **Cream Cheese Frosting**.

cream cheese frosting

- 1/2 cup butter, softened
- 1 (16-ounce) package confectioners sugar
- 2 teaspoons vanilla extract
- 1 (8-ounce) package cream cheese

Combine all ingredients, mixing until smooth. Frost cake when completely cooled.

. . . .

confectioners sugar pound cake

- 3/4 pound butter
- 1 (16-ounce) box confectioners sugar
- 6 eggs

- 1 teaspoon vanilla or lemon extract
- 2 cups sifted cake flour, plus 2 tablespoons

Cream butter and sugar until creamy and fluffy. Add eggs one at a time, beating well after each addition. Add vanilla or lemon extract. Add flour gradually and beat vigorously for 15 minutes. Pour into a well-greased and floured 10-inch tube pan. Bake at 275°F for 1 hour or until tests done.

. . . .

candy bar pound cake

1 cup butter
2 cups sugar
4 eggs
2-1/2 cups cake flour
1/4 teaspoon baking soda

1 cup buttermilk
1 cup chopped pecans
8 (1.55-ounce) Hershey® milk
   chocolate bars, melted
2 teaspoons vanilla extract

Cream butter until light and fluffy, gradually adding sugar.

Add eggs one at a time, beating well after each addition. (Dredge pecans in a small amount of flour until lightly coated). Sift flour and baking soda together and add alternately with buttermilk. Add melted chocolate bars, vanilla extract, and pecans.

Grease and flour a bundt or tube pan. Bake at 325°F for 1-1/2 hours or until tests done.

chocolate ripple pound cake

2 cups butter
2-1/2 cups sugar
10 eggs
1 tablespoon vanilla extract

1/4 teaspoon almond extract
4 cups cake flour
2 (1-ounce) squares unsweetened
   chocolate, melted

Cream butter and sugar until light and fluffy. Add eggs one at a time, blending well after each addition. Add vanilla and almond extracts and blend thoroughly. Add flour 1/2 cup at a time, beating well after each addition. Cream for 10 minutes. Grease and flour a 10-inch bundt or tube pan. Measure approximately 7 cups batter into pan. Into remaining batter, stir chocolate until well mixed. Spoon chocolate mixture over batter in bundt pan. With rubber spatula cut and twist through batter a few times for a marbleized effect.

Bake at 300°F for 1 hour and 30 minutes or until tests done. Cool cake in pan on wire rack 10 minutes; turn onto wire rack and cool completely.

Serve plain or with icing of your choice.

chocolate sour cream pound cake

1-1/2 cups butter, softened
3 cups sugar
6 large eggs
1 tablespoon vanilla extract
3 cups cake flour

1 teaspoon baking soda
1/8 teaspoon salt
1/2 cup cocoa
1 (8-ounce) carton sour cream
1 cup boiling water

Using an electric mixer on medium speed, cream butter and gradually add sugar. Beat until soft and fluffy, approximately 10 minutes. Add eggs one at a time, beating well after each addition. Stir in vanilla extract. Sift flour, baking soda, salt, and cocoa together. Add alternately with sour cream, beginning and ending with flour mixture. Add boiling water and mix well with a large spoon. Pour batter into a greased and floured 10-inch tube pan. Bake at 325°F for approximately 1 hour and 15 minutes or until tests done. Cool in pan on a wire rack for approximately 10 minutes. Remove and allow to cool completely. Delicious plain or with a chocolate glaze.

chocolate mocha pound cake

3 (1-ounce) squares unsweetened
   chocolate
1 tablespoon instant coffee granules
1 cup butter
2 cups sugar
4 eggs

3 cups cake flour
1 teaspoon salt
1 teaspoon baking powder
1 cup buttermilk
1 teaspoon vanilla extract
1 cup finely chopped pecans

Melt chocolate over hot water, stir in coffee granules; set aside.
   Cream together butter and sugar until light and fluffy. Add eggs one at a time, beating well after each addition. Sift flour, salt, and baking powder together and add to batter alternately with buttermilk. Stir in vanilla extract and chocolate mix-

ture, blending well. Stir in pecans. Bake at 325°F for 1 hour and 10 minutes or until tests done. When cooled, spread with **Chocolate Cream**.

chocolate cream

   4 ounces sweet chocolate
   2 ounces hot water
   1 tablespoon instant coffee granules
   1/4 cup whipping cream, whipped

Melt chocolate in 2 hot water and stir in coffee granules. Fold cool chocolate mixture into whipped cream.

. . . .

chocolate pound cake

1/2 cup butter	1/2 teaspoon baking powder
1/2 cup vegetable shortening	1/2 teaspoon salt
3 cups sugar	4 heaping tablespoons cocoa
5 eggs	1 cup milk
3 cups cake flour	1 tablespoon vanilla extract

Cream butter and vegetable shortening; add sugar gradually, beating well. Add eggs one at a time, beating well after each addition. Sift flour, baking powder, salt, and cocoa together. Add flour mixture alternately with milk. Add vanilla extract. Bake at 325°F for 1 hour and 40 minutes. When cooled completely, frost with **German Chocolate Frosting**.

. . . .

german chocolate frosting

1 stick butter
2 ounces German chocolate
1 (16-ounce) box confectioners sugar
Chopped pecans (optional)

Melt chocolate and butter over low heat, stirring constantly. Cool. Sift in confectioners sugar and blend well. Use evaporated milk to thin, if necessary. Add chopped pecans, if desired.

. . . .

chocolate chip pound cake

1-1/2 cups butter, softened
1-1/2 cups light brown sugar, well packed
1/2 cup granulated sugar
6 large eggs
3 cups cake flour
1 teaspoon baking soda
1 tablespoon vanilla extract
1 (8-ounce) carton sour cream
1 (6-ounce) package chocolate chips (dredge in a small amount of flour)

Using an electric mixer, beat butter until smooth. Gradually add sugars, beating until light and fluffy, approximately 10 minutes. Add eggs one at a time, beating well after each addition. Sift flour and baking soda together. Add alternately with sour cream, beginning and ending with flour mixture. Gently fold in chocolate chips thoroughly. Pour immediately into a greased and floured 10-inch tube pan. Bake at 325°F for approximately 1 hour and 15 minutes or until tests done. Cool in pan on a wire rack for approximately 10 minutes. Remove from pan and allow to cool.

. . . .

cinnamon sour cream pound cake

1 cup butter	1 (8-ounce) carton sour cream
2 cups sugar	1 teaspoon vanilla extract
2 eggs	1/2 cup sliced almonds, toasted
2-1/2 cups cake flour	1/2 teaspoon cinnamon
1 teaspoon baking powder	2 teaspoons sugar
1/2 teaspoon salt	

Cream butter; gradually add 2 cups sugar, beating until light and fluffy. Add eggs one at a time, beating well after each addition.

Sift flour, baking powder, and salt together 3 times. Add 1/3 flour mixture to creamed mixture alternately with half of the sour cream, stirring until well blended. Add vanilla extract, blending well.

Combine almonds, cinnamon, and remaining 2 tablespoons sugar; sprinkle 1/3 of mixture in a well-greased and floured 10-inch bundt pan. Pour in 1/2 of batter and sprinkle with another 1/3 of almond mixture. Pour remaining batter into pan and top with remaining almond mixture.

Bake at 350°F for 50 to 1 hour. Cool 1 hour before removing from pan.

coconut pound cake

1 cup butter	3 cups sifted cake flour
2 cups sugar	1 teaspoon baking powder
5 eggs	1/4 teaspoon salt
1 teaspoon lemon extract	1 cup milk
1/2 teaspoon vanilla extract	1-1/2 cups flaked coconut
Juice of 1 lemon	

Cream butter; add sugar gradually, beating until light and fluffy. Add eggs one at a time, beating well after each addition. Add lemon extract, vanilla extract, and lemon juice. Mix thoroughly.

Sift flour, baking powder, and salt together and add alternately with milk; fold in coconut.

Bake at 300°F for 1 hour and 15 minutes or until tests done. Serve plain or with **Buttermilk Icing.**

. . . .

buttermilk icing

1 cup buttermilk
2 cups sugar
1/2 cup butter

Combine and cook to soft ball stage (234°F to 240°F). Spread on cake.

. . . .

coconut lemon pound cake

1 cup butter, softened
1/2 cup solid vegetable shortening
3 cups granulated sugar
6 large eggs, separated
2 tablespoons freshly squeezed
lemon juice

1 teaspoon grated lemon zest
3 cups cake flour
1 cup whole milk
1 (3-1/2-ounce) can flaked coconut

Using an electric mixer, cream butter and shortening until smooth. Gradually add sugar, beating until light and fluffy. Add egg yolks one at a time, beating well after each addition. Stir in juice and zest. Sift flour 3 times, then gradually add to creamed mixture alternately with milk, beginning and ending with flour. Beat egg whites until stiff but not dry. Fold into batter, then fold in coconut. Pour into a greased and floured 10-inch tube pan or two loaf pans. Bake at 325°F for approximately 1 hour and 15 minutes or until tests done. Cool in pan on a wire rack for approximately 10 minutes before removing. Serve plain or glazed with **Coconut Lemon Glaze.**

coconut lemon glaze

1 cup granulated sugar
1/2 cup water
1 teaspoon pure lemon flavoring
1-1/2 teaspoons coconut flavoring

Combine sugar and water in a saucepan. Bring to a boil; add flavorings. Drizzle over warm cake and brush with a pastry brush for a smooth finish.

. . . .

cranberry pecan pound cake

1 cup butter
2 cups sugar
4 eggs
1 tablespoon vanilla extract
2-1/4 cups sifted cake flour
1/2 teaspoon baking powder

1/4 teaspoon salt
1/2 cup evaporated milk
1 cup chopped pecans
1 cup chopped raw cranberries
Confectioners sugar

Grease and flour a 10-inch tube or bundt pan; set aside.

Cream together butter and sugar until light and fluffy. Add eggs one at a time, beating well after each addition. Blend in vanilla extract. Sift flour, baking powder, and salt together and add to batter alternately with milk, fold in cranberries and pecans which have been lightly dredged in flour.

Bake at 325°F for 1 hour and 10 minutes or until tests done. Dust with confectioners sugar.

. . . .

cream cheese pound cake

- 3/4 pound butter
- 1 (8-ounces) package cream cheese, softened
- 3 cups sugar
- 6 egg yolks
- 3 cups cake flour
- 1 teaspoon vanilla extract
- 6 egg whites

Cream butter with cream cheese until soft and fluffy. Add sugar and beat well. Add egg yolks one at a time, until well blended. Sift flour and add gradually to batter, continuing to blend well. Stir in vanilla extract. Fold in stiffly beaten egg whites. Spoon into a well-buttered and floured tube pan.

Bake at 350°F for 1 hour or until tests done. Serve plain or glazed.

. . . .

elegant pound cake

For best results, do not substitute margarine for butter in this rich and luscious batter.

- 1 pound butter
- 2-2/3 cups sugar
- 8 eggs, separated
- 3-1/2 cups sifted cake flour
- 1/2 cup whipping cream
- 1 teaspoon vanilla extract

Lightly grease a very large tube pan; set aside. Cream butter thoroughly and add 2-1/3 cups sugar gradually; continue to cream, beating for approximately 10 minutes. Add egg yolks one at a time, beating well after each addition. Sift flour 3 times; add to batter alternately with cream and vanilla extract, beating for another 10 minutes until mixture is very light. Beat egg whites until very frothy and add 1/3 cup sugar gradually. Fold into creamed mixture by hand.

Pour batter into prepared pan. Bake at 300°F for 1 hour and 45 minutes or until tests done. Let cool in pan for 10 minutes before turning onto a wire rack to cool completely.

Serve plain or with **Lemon Glaze**. Also good with sweetened strawberries and whipped cream.

lemon glaze

1/2 cup confectioners sugar, sifted
   and firmly packed
1 teaspoon white corn syrup
2 teaspoons whipping cream

3 teaspoons lemon juice
1 teaspoon soft butter
Pinch of salt

Combine all ingredients and beat well to blend. Drizzle over top of cake. This icing adds flavor and helps to retain moisture.

. . . .

flavored pound cake

1-1/2 cups butter, softened
3 cups granulated sugar
6 large eggs
1 teaspoon each almond, butter,
   coconut, lemon, and vanilla extracts

3 cups cake flour
1 teaspoon baking powder
1 cup whole milk

With an electric mixer, cream butter and sugar until light and fluffy, approximately 10 minutes. Add eggs one at a time, beating well after each addition. Stir in extracts. Sift flour and baking powder together. Add to batter alternately with milk, beginning and ending with flour mixture. Pour into a greased and floured 10-inch tube pan or two loaf pans. Bake at 325°F for approximately 1 hour and 15 minutes or until tests done. Cool in pan on a wire rack for approximately 10 minutes before removing cake. Spoon **Flavored Glaze** over top of cake while cake is still warm.

flavored glaze

1 cup granulated sugar
1/2 cup water
1 teaspoon each almond, butter, coconut, lemon, and vanilla extracts

In a small saucepan, combine all ingredients. Bring to a boil, stirring until sugar is melted. Spoon hot mixture over warm cake.

. . . .

fruit pound cake

1 cup butter
1 (8-ounce) package cream cheese
1-1/2 cups sugar
4 eggs
2-1/2 cups cake flour, divided
1-1/2 teaspoons baking powder

1 cup chopped mixed candied fruit
1/2 cup golden seedless raisins
1/2 cup chopped dates
1/2 cup chopped pecans
Grated zest of 1 lemon
Confectioners sugar

Cream butter and cream cheese; gradually add sugar, beating well until light and fluffy. Add eggs one at a time, beating well after each addition.

Combine 1-3/4 cups flour and baking powder; gradually add to creamed mixture and beat until well blended. Dredge candied fruit, raisins, dates, pecans, and lemon zest with remaining 3/4 cup flour; stir to coat well. Stir mixture into batter.

Spoon into a greased and floured 10-inch tube pan. Bake at 325°F for approximately 1 hour and 20 minutes. Cool for 10 minutes; remove from pan. Dust with confectioners sugar. Garnish with candied cherries and candied pineapple slices, if desired.

. . . .

elegant sour cream pound cake

1/2 cup butter, softened
1/2 cup shortening
3 cups sugar
6 eggs, separated
3 cups sifted cake flour

1/4 teaspoon baking powder
1/4 teaspoon baking soda
1/4 teaspoon salt
1 cup sour cream

Cream butter and shortening; gradually add sugar, beating well. Add egg yolks one at a time, beating well after each addition.

Sift flour, baking powder, soda, and salt together; add to creamed mixture alternately with sour cream, beginning and ending with flour mixture. Beat egg whites until stiff peaks form; gently fold into batter. Pour into a greased and floured 10-inch tube pan. Bake at 325°F for 1 hour and 30 minutes or until tests done. Cool in pan for 10 minutes; remove from pan and cool completely.

. . . .

german chocolate pound cake

1 cup butter
2 cups sugar
4 eggs
2 teaspoons vanilla extract
2 teaspoons butter flavoring

1 cup buttermilk
3 cups flour, sifted
1 teaspoon salt
1/2 teaspoon baking soda
1 package German sweet chocolate

Cream butter and sugar; add eggs one at a time, beating well after each addition. Add vanilla extract, butter flavoring, and buttermilk. Sift flour, salt, and baking soda together 3 times. Melt chocolate in top of double boiler. Add dry ingredients alternately to first mixture with chocolate. Mix well. Pour into a large well-greased tube pan. Bake at 300°F for 1 hour and 30 minutes or until cake pulls away from sides of pan. Remove from oven and cover tightly with plastic wrap until cool. Frost with **Chocolate Frosting**.

chocolate frosting

1/4 cup butter
4 tablespoons cocoa
1 teaspoon vanilla extract
1 (16-ounce) box confectioners sugar
Brewed coffee

Cream butter until light and fluffy, add sugar. Add cocoa and vanilla extract. Use enough hot coffee to make spreadable.

. . . .

ginger pound cake

1 cup butter
2 cups light brown sugar, packed
4 eggs, separated
3-1/4 cups cake flour
1 teaspoon baking powder
1 teaspoon nutmeg

1 tablespoon ground ginger
1 teaspoon salt
1/2 cup whipping cream
2 tablespoons minced candied
   ginger (optional)

Grease a tube pan and line with wax paper.
   Cream butter and sugar well. Add egg yolks one at a time, beating well after each addition. Sift dry ingredients together and add to batter alternately with cream. Fold in candied ginger, if used, and egg whites beaten stiff, but not dry. Pour batter gently into tube pan. Bake at 325°F for 1 hour or until tests done.
   Serve plain or with a butter cream glaze, if desired.

. . . .

lemon pound cake

1 stick butter
1/2 cup vegetable shortening
2 cups sugar
3 eggs
3 cups cake flour

1/2 teaspoon baking soda
1/4 teaspoon salt
1 cup buttermilk
1 tablespoon lemon juice
1 tablespoon grated lemon zest

Cream butter, vegetable shortening, and sugar together until light and fluffy. Add eggs one at a time, beating well after each addition. Sift flour, baking soda, and salt together and add to batter alternately with buttermilk, lemon juice, and lemon zest. Pour into a greased and floured bundt or tube pan. Bake at 325°F for approximately 1 hour or until tests done. Cool 5 minutes in pan. Turn onto a wire rack and cool completely. Cover entire cake with **Lemon Icing**.

lemon icing

1 stick butter
Juice and zest of 2 lemons
1 (16-ounce) box confectioners sugar

Cream butter until smooth. Add confectioners sugar until well blended. Add juice and lemon zest. Blend thoroughly and spread on cake immediately.

moroccan pound cake

2/3 cup butter
1/2 cup vegetable shortening
2 cups sugar
4 eggs
3-1/2 cups cake flour
3 teaspoons baking powder
1/4 teaspoon salt
1 cup milk

1 teaspoon vanilla extract
1/2 cup raisins
3/4 cup chopped unsalted mixed
  nuts
1 tablespoon cocoa
1 tablespoon cinnamon
Confectioners sugar

Cream butter, vegetable shortening, and sugar until light and fluffy. Add eggs one at a time, beating well after each addition. Sift flour, baking powder, and salt together. Add to batter alternately with milk and vanilla extract, beating well. Fold in raisins and nuts. Grease and line the bottom of a 10-inch tube pan with wax paper. Pour 3/4 of the batter into prepared pan. Sift cocoa and cinnamon together and mix into remaining batter. Spoon batter into pan and run a knife through batter several times to marbleize. Bake at 325°F for 1 hour and 15 minutes or until tests done. Let stand 5 minutes and turn onto a wire rack. Peel off wax paper. Cool and sprinkle with confectioners sugar.

. . . .

lemon gelatin pound cake

1 box lemon cake mix
1 (3-ounce) box lemon-flavored gelatin
4 eggs
1 cup milk
3/4 cup vegetable oil

Mix together cake mix, gelatin, eggs, and milk. Add oil and mix well. Bake at 350°F for 1 hour in a tube pan or until tests done. Spread **Lemon Icing** over cake.

lemon icing

3 tablespoons butter, softened   Juice of 2 lemons
1-1/4 cups confectioners sugar

Mix all ingredients well and pour over cake while it is still hot.

. . . .

million dollar pound cake

1 pound butter   4 cups cake flour
3 cups sugar   3/4 cup milk
6 eggs   2 teaspoons vanilla extract

Cream butter and sugar until light and fluffy. Add eggs one at a time, creaming well
after each addition. Add flour alternately with milk, beating well. Stir in vanilla
extract. Pour into a well-greased and floured 10-inch tube pan. Bake at 325°F for 1
hour and 15 minutes or longer, if necessary.

. . . .

mrs. walker's pound cake

2 sticks butter, plus 1 stick   3 cups sifted plain flour
   margarine   1-1/2 teaspoons vanilla extract
2 cups sugar   (or 2 teaspoons lemon flavoring)
6 eggs

Beat butter and sugar until light and fluffy. Add eggs one at a time, beating well
after each addition. Add flour to batter alternatively with extract or flavoring. Pour
batter into greased and floured tube pan. Bake at 325°F for approximately 1 hour
and 10 minutes, or until cake leaves sides of pan. Cool slightly in pan, before turning onto wire rack to finish cooling.

. . . .

peach pound cake

2 cups granulated sugar
1-1/2 cups vegetable oil
4 large eggs
2 teaspoons vanilla extract

3 cups sifted self-rising flour
1 cup chopped pecans
3 cups fresh ripe peaches, pared and
diced

Using an electric mixer, combine sugar and oil. Beat until mixture is well blended.
Add eggs one at a time, beating well after each addition. Stir in vanilla extract.
Gradually add sifted flour until mixed thoroughly. Do not overbeat. Dredge pecans
in a small amount of flour and fold into batter. Fold in peaches. Pour into a greased
and floured 10-inch bundt pan or 2 loaf pans. Bake at 325°F for 1 hour or until
tests done. Cool in pan on a wire rack for approximately 5 minutes before removing.
Cool completely. Frost cake with **Peach Frosting**.

peach frosting

1 (3-ounce) package cream cheese,
softened

1-1/2 cups sifted confectioners sugar
2 tablespoons fresh peach puree

Using an electric mixer, beat cream cheese until smooth. Gradually add confectioners sugar, followed by peach puree. Beat until well combined. Spread over top and
on sides of cooled cake.

pecan pound cake

1 cup butter, softened
3 cups sugar
6 eggs, separated
3 cups sifted cake flour

1/4 teaspoon baking soda
1 cup sour cream
2 to 4 cups chopped pecans

Cream butter and sugar until light and fluffy. Add egg yolks one at a time, beating well after each addition. Set aside approximately 1/3 cup flour. Combine remaining flour and baking soda; add to creamed mixture alternately with sour cream, beating well after each addition. Fold in stiffly beaten egg whites. Dredge pecans in reserved flour and fold into batter.

Spoon batter into a greased and floured 10-inch tube pan. Bake at 300°F for 1 hour and 30 minutes. Cool 15 minutes before removing from pan.

. . . .

pineapple pound cake

2 cups vegetable shortening
3 cups sugar
9 eggs

3 cups sifted cake flour
1 (8-1/4-ounce) can crushed
pineapple, undrained

Cream shortening well, gradually add sugar, beating well.

Add eggs one at a time, beating well after each addition. Add sifted flour to batter alternately with pineapple and juice. Grease lightly and put wax paper in bottom of a large tube pan. Pour batter into prepared pan. Bake at 350°F for 1 hour and 30 minutes or until tests done. While cake is still warm, drizzle with **Pineapple Glaze**.

pineapple glaze

1-1/2 cups confectioners sugar
1 (8-1/4-ounce) can crushed pineapple, undrained
1/4 stick melted butter

Mix all ingredients well and drizzle over warm cake.

. . . .

old fashioned pound cake

1 pound butter
1 pound sugar
9 eggs, separated

1 teaspoon lemon extract
1 pound flour (4-1/2 cups, sifted)

Cream butter and sugar until light and fluffy. Add egg yolks one at a time, beating well after each addition. Add lemon extract. Add flour gradually, beating well after each addition. Fold in stiffly beaten egg whites. Pour batter into a well-greased tube pan. Bake for 1 hour at 325°F or until tests done.

· · · · · · · ·

orange sour cream pound cake

1 cup butter, softened
2 cups granulated sugar
4 large eggs
3 tablespoons freshly squeezed
   orange juice
2 tablespoons grated orange zest
3 cups cake flour

3 tablespoons powdered whipped
   topping mix
1 1/2 teaspoons baking powder
1 1/2 teaspoons baking soda
1 (8-ounce) carton sour cream
1/2 cup coarsely chopped pecans

Using an electric mixer, cream butter and sugar until light and fluffy, approximately 10 minutes. Add eggs one at a time, beating just until yolk is incorporated after each addition. Stir in orange juice and orange zest. Sift flour, whipped topping mix, baking powder, and baking soda together. Add alternately with sour cream, beginning and ending with flour mixture. Dredge pecans in a small amount of flour and fold into batter. Pour into a greased and floured tube pan or 2 loaf pans. Bake at 325°F for approximately 1 hour or until tests done. Cool in pan on a wire rack for approximately 10 minutes. Remove from pan and cool on a wire rack. Serve warm or cold.

· · · · · · · ·

original pound cake

Classic pound cake recipes call for equal pound amounts of all ingredients. Use the empty confectioners sugar box as a quick and precise way to measure the cake flour.

1 pound butter
1 pound confectioners sugar
12 eggs, separated
1 pound flour (4-1/2 cups, sifted)

1/2 teaspoon nutmeg
1/2 cup whipping cream
1/4 cup grated lemon peel

Cream butter and sugar; add egg yolks, beating well after each addition. Sift together flour and nutmeg, add to batter alternately with cream. Fold in lemon peel and stiffly beaten egg whites. Bake at 325°F for 1 hour or until tests done.

. . . .

peanut butter pound cake no. 1

1 cup butter
2 cups granulated sugar
1 cup light brown sugar, packed
1/2 cup creamy peanut butter
5 eggs
1 tablespoon vanilla extract

3 cups cake flour
1/2 teaspoon baking powder
1/2 teaspoon salt
1/4 teaspoon baking soda
1 cup milk

Cream butter and granulated sugar until light and fluffy. Add brown sugar and peanut butter and continue beating thoroughly. Add eggs one at a time, beating well after each addition. Add vanilla extract and blend well.

Sift dry ingredients together and add to batter alternately with milk. Pour into a large lightly greased tube pan. Bake at 325°F for approximately 1 hour or until tests done. Frost with **Peanut Butter Frosting**, if desired.

peanut butter frosting

1/2 stick butter
Pinch of salt
1 ounce milk
2 eggs

1/3 cup creamy peanut butter
1 (16-ounce) box confectioners
sugar

Combine all ingredients and beat until smooth. Be careful not to use too much milk, add just enough to make frosting spreadable.

. . . .

peanut butter pound cake no. 2

2-1/2 sticks butter
2 cups sugar
6 eggs
1 teaspoon vanilla extract
1/2 cup creamy or crunchy peanut
butter

2 cups cake flour
1 teaspoon baking powder
1/4 teaspoon salt
1/3 cup finely chopped peanuts

Cream together butter and sugar until fluffy. Beat in eggs one at a time, beating well after each addition. Add vanilla extract. Slowly beat in peanut butter. Sift together flour, baking powder, and salt. Add to batter in small amounts, blending well after each addition. Spoon batter into a lightly greased tube pan. Bake at 350°F for 45 minutes; reduce heat to 325°F and bake an additional 15 to 20 minutes, or until tests done. If desired, toward end of baking time and while batter is still soft, sprinkle with chopped peanuts to give cake a crunchy topping.

. . . .

pineapple crush pound cake

1 cup butter, softened
1 cup vegetable shortening
3 cups granulated sugar
8 large eggs

1 teaspoon vanilla extract
3 cups cake flour
1 (8-1/4-ounce) can crushed
  pineapple, in heavy syrup

Using an electric mixer, beat butter and shortening until mixture is creamed well. Gradually add sugar, mixing thoroughly, approximately 10 minutes. Add eggs one at a time, beating just until yolk is incorporated after each addition. Stir in extract. Sift flour, measure and resift 3 times. Slowly add flour, beating until batter is smooth and blended. Fold in pineapple and juice, mixing thoroughly. Pour into a greased and floured 10-inch tube pan. Bake at 300°F for approximately 1 hour and 15 minutes or until tests done. Cool in pan on a wire rack for approximately 10 minutes. Remove from pan and drizzle with **Orange Juice Glaze** while cake is still warm.

orange juice glaze

1 (16-ounce) box confectioner sugar, sifted
1/2 cup freshly squeezed orange juice

Using an electric mixer, combine confectioners sugar and orange juice. Beat until mixture is smooth. Spoon 1/2 of the mixture over cake while cake is still warm. Cool cake completely and drizzle with remaining glaze.

. . . .

pecan crunch pound cake

1-1/2 cups butter, softened
1 (16-ounce) box confectioners
    sugar, sifted
6 large eggs

1 tablespoon vanilla extract
3 cups cake flour
1 cup pecans, toasted and chopped

Using an electric mixer, cream butter until smooth. Gradually add confectioners sugar, beating until soft and fluffy, approximately 10 minutes. Add eggs one at a time, beating just until yolk is incorporated after each addition. Stir in vanilla extract. Sift flour 3 times and gradually add to creamed mixture. Toast pecans, then coarsely chop them in a food processor. Dredge pecans in a small amount of flour and fold into batter well. Pour immediately into a greased and floured 10-inch tube pan. Bake at 325°F for approximately 1 hour and 10 minutes or until tests done. Cool in pan on a wire rack for approximately 10 minutes. Remove and cool completely on a wire rack.

praline pecan pound cake

1 cup butter, softened
1/2 cup vegetable shortening
1 (16-ounce) box light brown sugar
5 large eggs
1 tablespoon vanilla extract

3 cups cake flour
1/4 teaspoon baking powder
1 cup whole milk
2 cups chopped pecans
Confectioners sugar

Using an electric mixer, cream butter and shortening until smooth. Gradually add sugar, beating until light and fluffy. Add eggs one at a time, beating well after each addition. Stir in vanilla extract. Sift flour and baking powder together. Add flour mixture to batter alternately with milk, beginning and ending with flour mixture. Dredge pecans in a small amount of flour and fold into batter thoroughly. Pour into a greased and floured 10-inch tube pan or 2 loaf pans. Bake at 325°F for approximately 1 hour and 15 minutes or until tests done. Cool in pan on a wire rack for approximately 10 minutes before removing cake. Dust cake with confectioners sugar while cake is warm.

red velvet pound cake

1-1/2 cups butter, softened
1/2 cup vegetable shortening
3 cups granulated sugar
8 large eggs
1 tablespoon vanilla extract

1 (1-ounce) bottle red food coloring
1 teaspoon white vinegar
3 cups cake flour
1/4 teaspoon baking soda
1 cup buttermilk

Using an electric mixer, cream butter and shortening until smooth. Gradually add sugar and beat until light and fluffy, approximately 10 minutes. Add eggs one at a time, beating well after each addition. Stir in vanilla extract, food coloring, and vinegar, blending well. Sift flour and baking soda together. Add alternately with buttermilk, beginning and ending with flour mixture. Pour into a greased and floured 10-inch tube pan or 2 loaf pans. Bake at 325°F for approximately 1 hour and 15 minutes or until tests done. Cool in pan on a wire rack for approximately 10 minutes before removing cake. Cool completely. Frost with **Cream Cheese Frosting**.

cream cheese frosting

1/2 cup butter, softened
1 (8-ounce) package cream cheese, softened
1 (16-ounce) box confectioners sugar
1/2 teaspoon vanilla extract
1 cup chopped pecans

Using an electric mixer, cream butter and cream cheese until smooth and fluffy. Gradually add confectioners sugar until blended. Stir in vanilla extract. Add pecans and mix thoroughly. Spread over cooled cake.

. . . .

sour cream pound cake

1/2 pound butter, softened
3 cups sugar
6 large eggs
3 cups flour
1/4 teaspoon baking soda

1/4 teaspoon salt
1 (8-ounce) carton sour cream
1 to 2 teaspoons vanilla extract or
    lemon extract

Measure flour and sift 3 times. Cream butter well. Add sugar to butter gradually, creaming thoroughly. Add eggs one at a time, beating well after each addition. Add flour, baking soda, and salt alternately to batter with sour cream. Add vanilla or lemon extract. Bake at 325°F for 1 hour and 30 minutes. Do not open oven door during baking or cake will fall.

. . . .

sweet potato pound cake

1/2 cup vegetable shortening
1/2 cup butter, softened
2 cups sugar
6 eggs
3-1/2 cups cake flour
1/2 teaspoon salt
1/4 teaspoon baking soda

1 teaspoon baking powder
1 cup buttermilk
1 cup pureed cooked sweet potatoes
1/2 teaspoon coconut extract
1/4 cup slivered almonds, toasted
    and finely chopped
1/4 cup flaked coconut

Cream shortening and butter; gradually add sugar, beating until light and fluffy. Add eggs one at a time, beating well after each addition. Sift flour, salt, baking soda, and baking powder together and add to batter alternately with buttermilk. Stir in sweet potatoes and coconut extract until well blended.

Grease and flour a 12-cup bundt pan; sprinkle almonds and coconut evenly over bottom. Pour batter into pan. Bake at 350°F for 1 hour or until tests done. Cool in pan for 10 minutes; remove and cool completely.

. . . .

white pound cake

1 cup butter, softened
2 cups granulated sugar
8 egg whites, unbeaten
1 teaspoon lemon extract or 1
   teaspoon vanilla extract

3 cups cake flour
1 teaspoon baking powder
1/2 teaspoon salt
1 cup whole milk

Using an electric mixer, cream butter and sugar together until light and fluffy. Add egg whites in 3 portions, lightly beating after each addition. Stir in lemon or vanilla extract. Sift flour, baking powder, and salt together. Add to batter alternately with milk, beginning and ending with flour mixture. Pour into a greased and floured 10-inch tube pan or 2 loaf pans. Bake at 325°F for approximately 1 hour and 15 minutes or until tests done. Cool in pan on a wire rack for approximately 10 minutes before removing cake to rack to cool completely.

. . . .

yogurt pound cake

1 cup butter, softened
2 cups granulated sugar
6 large eggs
1 teaspoon vanilla extract
3 cups cake flour

1/2 teaspoon baking soda
1/4 teaspoon salt
1 (8-ounce) carton peach, strawberry, or black cherry yogurt

Using an electric mixer, cream butter and sugar together until light and fluffy. Add eggs one at a time, beating well after each addition. Stir in vanilla extract. Sift flour, baking soda, and salt together. Add to batter alternately with yogurt, beginning and ending with flour mixture. Pour into a greased and floured 10-inch tube pan. Bake at 325°F for 1 hour and 15 minutes or until tests done. Cool in pan on a wire rack for approximately 10 minutes before removing cake to rack to cool completely.

. . . .

refrigerator
cakes
&
desserts

Don't wait for a birthday to bake a cake... Celebrate your loved ones— and yourself— everyday!

angel food delight

Angel food cake or approximately 30 ladyfingers
1 (3-ounce) package orange-flavored gelatin
1 cup water
1 (8-1/4-ounce) can crushed pineapple, drained

1 (15-1/4-ounce) can sliced peaches, drained and chopped
12 maraschino cherries, chopped
2 heaping cups of miniature marshmallows
1 pint whipping cream, whipped

Line a 9 x 12-inch glass baking dish with sliced angel food cake or ladyfingers. Set gelatin with 1 cup water. Combine fruits and marshmallows. Whip cream; fold into fruit mixture and gelatin. Pour over cake. Chill overnight.

angel's surprise

4 egg yolks
1 cup sugar
1 pint milk
2 tablespoons flour
Pinch of salt
1 envelope unflavored gelatin
1/2 cup cold water

4 egg whites, beaten stiff
1/2 pint whipping cream, whipped
1 teaspoon almond extract
Angel Food cake
1/2 pint whipping cream
Toasted slivered almonds

Combine egg yolks, sugar, milk, flour, and salt and cook until ingredients thicken into a custard. Dissolve gelatin in cold water. Add to custard and cool. Beat egg whites until stiff peaks form. Add egg whites and whipped cream to custard mixture. Add extract.

Break angel food cake into large pieces and put in oblong glass baking dish. Pour custard over cake. Refrigerate overnight. Garnish with 1/2 pint of whipped cream and toasted slivered almonds.

blueberry glaze cake

1 (12-ounce) box vanilla wafers
1 stick margarine
1 package whipped topping
1 (8-ounce) package cream cheese,
    softened

1 cup sugar
1 (21-ounce can) blueberry pie
    filling

Crush vanilla wafers. Melt margarine and mix with wafers. Press in bottom of glass baking dish, reserving 1/2 cup for topping. Prepare dessert topping as directed. Mix together cream cheese and sugar, blending well. Add dessert topping.

Spread 1/2 of this mixture over crust and cover with pie filling. Spread remaining dessert topping mixture on top. Refrigerate overnight.

buttercream satin cake

Pound cake, angel food cake, or
    approximately 30 ladyfingers
1/2 cup butter
1 cup confectioners sugar

4 egg yolks
1 tablespoon vanilla extract
4 egg whites
1 pint whipping cream, whipped

Line a mold or a large bowl with pound cake or angel food cake pieces or ladyfingers.

Cream butter; beat in sugar until fluffy. Beat in egg yolks one at a time, beating well after each addition. Add vanilla extract and fold in stiffly beaten egg whites. Put filling and remaining cake in bowl alternately in layers. Chill 12 hours or longer before serving.

charlotte cake

1 quart whipping cream	1 cup cold water
1 cup sugar	1 cup sherry
4 egg whites	1/2 pint whipping cream
2 tablespoons plain gelatin	Almonds and crystallized cherries

Whip 1 quart whipping cream until it is about half as stiff as desired, then add 1 cup sugar and continue to whip. Beat egg whites until foamy and add to whipped cream, folding in carefully. Dissolve gelatin in 1 cup cold water. Let stand until approximately the consistency of applesauce; then dissolve over very low heat or in top of double boiler. Let stand until it is cool.

Add gelatin very slowly, stirring carefully, to whipped cream and finally add sherry slowly. Line with ladyfingers an angel food cake pan with a removable bottom and pour mixture in slowly. Chill in refrigerator for at least 2 hours.

Unmold on serving platter. Garnish with 1/2 pint cream, whipped with crystallized cherries and almonds.

. . . .

chocolate coconut icebox cake

4 (1-ounce) squares unsweetened chocolate	2 dozen coconut macaroons, crumbled
8 eggs, separated	Ladyfingers
1/2 cup cold water	1 cup chopped pecans
1 cup sugar, divided	1 teaspoon vanilla extract
1-1/2 sticks butter, softened	1/2 pint whipping cream, whipped
2 cups confectioners sugar	

Melt chocolate in top of double boiler. Beat egg yolks and add 1/2 cup sugar. Add water and blend with chocolate. Cook until very thick, stirring constantly. Fold in stiffly beaten egg whites into which has been beaten 1/2 cup sugar. Chill in refrigerator.

Cream butter and gradually add confectioners sugar, pecans, flavoring, and macaroon crumbs. Combine two mixtures. Line bottom and sides of springform pan with split ladyfingers. Pour mixture into pan. Chill in refrigerator overnight. Serve with sweetened whipped cream.

chocolate loaf cake

1 small sponge cake, bought or
   homemade; or 20 ladyfingers
4 ounces chocolate
1/2 cup milk
1/2 cup sugar

4 eggs, separated
1 teaspoon vanilla extract
1/4 teaspoon salt
1 cup whipping cream, whipped
1/4 cup confectioners sugar

Line small loaf pan with wax paper. Cover bottom and sides with thin slices of sponge cake or ladyfingers. Melt chocolate over hot water. Add milk and continue cooking over hot water until smooth and blended, stirring constantly. Add sugar to slightly beaten yolks and add chocolate mixture slowly, stirring constantly.

Cook until thickened and smooth. Remove from heat and while still hot, fold in stiffly beaten egg whites. Add 1/2 teaspoon vanilla extract and salt. Pour half of chocolate mixture into cake-lined pan. Cover with a layer of sponge cake, add remaining chocolate mixture and cover with last layer of cake slices.

Chill for 12 hours or overnight. Turn out onto cake plate. Cover with whipped cream flavored with confectioners sugar and 1/2 teaspoon vanilla extract.

chocolate-filled angel cake

1 large angel food cake
3 cups whipping cream
6 tablespoons cocoa
6 tablespoons sugar

1/8 teaspoon salt
1 cup sliced, blanched and toasted
   almonds

Cut a slice approximately 1-inch thick from top of cake. Remove center from cake, leaving walls and bottom approximately 1-inch thick. Mix cocoa, sugar, and salt with cream and chill for 1 hour. Whip cream mixture stiff and add 1/2 cup almonds. Fill cake with 1/3 of cocoa mixture. Place top on cake and frost with remaining cocoa mixture. Sprinkle remaining almonds over cake. Chill 2 to 3 hours before serving.

caramel gingersnaps

1 (14-ounce) can sweetened condensed milk
2 dozen gingersnaps
Candied ginger, cut fine

Place can of sweetened condensed milk in a saucepan of boiling water and keep at boiling point for 3 hours. Be extremely cautious to keep can well covered with water. Cool can before opening.

Beat caramelized milk until smooth and creamy. Spread on gingersnaps. Stack 4 gingersnaps on top of each other. Spread top and sides of each stack with caramelized milk. Decorate with candied ginger. Chill and refrigerate 8 hours or longer.

chantilly sponge cake

1 large sponge cake
1 cup cubed or crushed pineapple, drained
12 marshmallows, quartered

1 cup cut strawberries
1/2 teaspoon vanilla extract
2 cups whipping cream, whipped
20 large whole strawberries

Cut cool sponge cake into two layers. Fold pineapple, marshmallows, strawberries, and vanilla extract into whipped cream. Spread bottom layer liberally with the mixed filling. Cover with the top layer and spread remaining mixture over top and sides. Chill for 2 to 3 hours before serving. Garnish with whole berries.

coffee almond cake

1/2 pound butter, softened
1/2 cup sugar
5 egg yolks
1/3 cup toasted almonds, pulverized
2 teaspoons vanilla extract

1/2 cup strong cold coffee
1-1/2 dozen ladyfingers, split
1 pint whipping cream
Slivered toasted almonds, for garnish

Cream butter and sugar thoroughly. Add egg yolks one at a time, beating well after each addition. Add pulverized almonds and vanilla extract and blend. Add coffee gradually and beat until smooth. Line a 2-quart mold with ladyfingers. Spread half the coffee mixture on top, then a layer of ladyfingers. Spread with other half of mixture and a final layer of ladyfingers. Chill overnight. Invert and spread sweetened whipped cream evenly over top. Sprinkle with slivered almonds.

colonial english trifle

1 (15-1/4-ounce) can peeled, pitted
  apricots
1 sponge cake, cut into 2 layers
3 tablespoons strawberry jam
1/2 pound macaroons, crumbled
1 cup sherry
1-1/2 cups milk

3 eggs
1 tablespoon sugar
1/4 teaspoon salt
Pinch of vanilla extract
Chopped pecans
1/2 pint heavy cream

Line deep, round glass casserole with drained apricots. Top with layer of sponge cake. Spread with jam. Top with remaining cake layer and macaroons. Pour sherry on top.

Scald milk in double boiler. Beat eggs with sugar and salt. Add to milk and stir until custard is slightly thickened. Cool 15 minutes and add vanilla extract. Pour custard over cake mixture. Chill until set or overnight. Top with whipped cream and nuts before serving.

date and nut roll

2 cups vanilla wafer crumbs
1 cup chopped dates
1/2 cup chopped pecans

1/2 cup sweetened condensed milk
2 teaspoons lemon juice

Combine vanilla wafer crumbs, dates, and nuts. Blend condensed milk and lemon juice together. Add to crumb mixture and knead well. Form into a roll 3 inches in diameter and wrap in wax paper. Chill 12 hours. Cut into slices and serve with whipped cream topping or hard sauce flavored with brandy.

. . . .

delicious butterscotch cake

1 tablespoon unflavored gelatin
1/4 cup cold water
2-1/2 tablespoons butter
2/3 cup brown sugar
1-1/2 cups milk
2 eggs, separated

1/4 teaspoon salt
1 cup whipping cream, whipped and chilled
1/2 teaspoon vanilla extract
1 dozen ladyfingers

Soften gelatin in water for 5 minutes. Melt butter, add sugar and cook together until well blended. Add milk, heat and pour over well-beaten egg yolks, stirring constantly. Add salt and cook over hot water until mixture coats a spoon, stirring constantly.

Remove from heat and add softened gelatin. Stir until dissolved, then chill until mixture begins to thicken. Fold in stiffly beaten egg whites, whipped cream, and vanilla extract. Pour into a mold lined with separated ladyfingers. Chill until firm.

. . . .

festive orange delight

2 envelopes unflavored gelatin
1 cup water
8 eggs, separated
1/2 teaspoon salt
2 (6-ounce) cans orange juice concentrate, thawed

Grated zest of 1 orange
1 cup sugar
1/2 pint whipping cream, whipped
Mandarin oranges, toasted almonds,
and whipped cream for garnish

Dissolve gelatin in water in top of a double boiler. Beat egg yolks and add salt. Add yolks to gelatin mixture and beat thoroughly. Place over boiling water and cook, stirring constantly, until mixture begins to thicken. Remove from heat and add orange juice concentrate and zest. Chill until slightly thickened. Whip egg whites until foamy, gradually add sugar and beat until stiff. Whip cream and fold both mixtures into orange mixture. Pour mixture into a buttered dish and chill at least 8 hours. When ready to serve, garnish with almonds, Mandarin oranges, and sweetened whipped cream, if desired.

elegant ladyfinger dessert

1/2 pound butter, softened
1 cup sifted confectioners sugar
6 eggs

1 (16-ounce) can crushed pineapple,
drained
32 to 34 ladyfingers

Cream butter until very light and fluffy; add sugar gradually, beating well after each addition. Add egg yolks one at a time, beating well after each addition. Add pineapple. Beat egg whites until stiff but not dry; fold into batter.

Split ladyfingers into 2 layers and place a layer in a glass baking dish. Cover with 1/2 of mixture, then remaining ladyfingers. Top with remaining mixture and cover. Refrigerate at least 24 hours before serving. Serve topped with whipped cream.

frozen strawberry delight

2 (3-ounce) packages strawberry gelatin
2 cups hot water
1 (10-ounce) package frozen strawberries, slightly thawed; or 1 pint fresh
    strawberries, sweetened to taste
1 angel food cake
1/2 gallon vanilla ice cream, slightly softened
1 (10-ounce) carton dessert topping

Dissolve gelatin in water. Add strawberries. Tear angel food cake into bite-size pieces and place in bottom of greased tube pan. Add a layer of softened ice cream and a layer of dessert topping. Repeat these layers 3 times. Punch holes in cake and pour gelatin mixture over cake. Place in freezer. When ready to serve, dip pan in hot water and remove cake to serving plate. Garnish with fresh strawberries.

heavenly fruit cake

1 pound package marshmallows, cut up
1 pound graham crackers, rolled into fine crumbs
1 pound pecans, chopped
1 (16-ounce) box raisins
1 pound English walnuts, chopped
1/2 pound cherries, cut up
1/2 pound mixed nuts, chopped
1 cup grated coconut
1 can sweetened condensed milk

Mix marshmallows and graham crackers. Blend mixture well with remaining ingredients. Place in a foil-lined pan and refrigerate at least 24 hours.

floating island

3 cups milk
4 egg yolks
1/2 cup sugar
1-1/2 tablespoons cornstarch
Pinch of salt
1 teaspoon vanilla extract

Sponge cake or ladyfingers
1 tablespoon sherry flavoring
1/2 pint whipped cream, sweetened
1 cup chopped blanched almonds
Strawberry jelly, optional

In top of double boiler, scald milk. Beat egg yolks until thick, beat in sugar, cornstarch, and salt. Gradually beat hot milk into egg mixture. Return milk to double boiler and cook until mixture thickens. Stir in vanilla extract.

Cover bottom of large bowl with broken cake pieces or ladyfingers. Sprinkle with sherry flavoring and pour custard over all. Top generously with sweetened whipped cream and, if desired, dollops of strawberry jelly. Serve from the bowl.

. . . .

frozen strawberry cake

1-1/2 cups crushed fresh strawberries
2/3 cup sugar
1 tablespoon lemon juice, freshly
   squeezed

3 cups graham cracker crumbs
1/2 cup whipping cream
1-1/2 teaspoons vanilla extract

Combine ingredients in order listed and blend well. Line an oblong pan with parchment paper. Fill pan with the mixture and freeze until firm. Cut into squares, top with sweetened whipped cream and chopped pecans, if desired.

. . . .

macaroon delight

12 almond macaroons
4 egg whites
4 egg yolks
3/4 cup sugar
1/2 cup sherry
1 pint whipping cream, whipped

Leave macaroons out overnight or place in warm oven for a few minutes to dry. Roll out macaroons to make crumb mixture. Beat egg whites until stiff. In a separate bowl, beat egg yolks and gradually add sugar and sherry. Fold in stiffly beaten egg whites.

Line buttered serving dish with half the macaroon crumbs. Pour mixture on top and sprinkle remaining crumbs over top. Freeze until ready to serve.

holiday cake

2 tablespoons unflavored gelatin
1 quart milk
2 eggs, separated
3/4 cup sugar
1/4 teaspoon salt
3/4 cup chopped maraschino cherries

1/3 cup maraschino syrup
1 teaspoon vanilla extract
1-1/2 cups whipping cream, whipped and sweetened
2 dozen vanilla wafers

Soften gelatin in 1/2 cup milk. In double boiler, scald remaining milk and pour over beaten egg yolks. Add sugar, salt, and softened gelatin; return to double boiler; cook until mixture coats a spoon. Cool. Add cherries, juice, and vanilla extract. Chill until mixture begins to thicken.

Fold in beaten egg whites and half the whipped cream. Butter a cake pan and arrange vanilla wafers around the inside of the pan. Pour in filling and cover top with remaining vanilla wafers. Chill overnight. Unmold and frost sides and top of cake with remaining whipped cream.

lemonade loaf

1 angel food loaf
1 (6-ounce) can pink lemonade
concentrate, thawed
1 quart vanilla ice cream, well
softened

1 cup heavy cream, whipped
(optional)

Slice cake lengthwise in 3 even layers. Stir ice cream to soften. With spoon, zigzag lemonade concentrate through ice cream until marbled. Spread ice cream mixture between cake layers. Freeze approximately 1 hour. Before serving, spread top and sides of loaf with whipped cream.

Whipped cream frosting may be omitted, in which case the top layer of the cake should be frosted with part of the ice cream and lemonade mixture.

lemon bisque

1 (3-ounce) package lemon gelatin
1-1/4 cups hot water
1/2 cup sugar
4 tablespoons lemon juice, freshly
squeezed

Grated zest of 1 lemon
Pinch of salt
1 (13-ounce) can evaporated milk,
chilled
2 cups vanilla wafer crumbs

Dissolve gelatin in hot water. Put sugar, lemon juice, zest, and salt in pan and heat until thoroughly dissolved. Add softened gelatin to hot mixture. Cool. Whip evaporated milk until stiff peaks form. Fold gelatin mixture gradually into cream. Butter a square glass baking dish and sprinkle with 2/3 of the wafer crumbs. Press crumbs to set. Pour bisque into dish and sprinkle top with remaining crumbs. Place in refrigerator at least 6 hours. Best made the day before it is to be served. May be garnished with fresh strawberries.

lemon charlotte

1 envelope gelatin
1/2 cup cold water
4 eggs, separated
1 cup sugar, divided
Pinch of salt
1/2 cup lemon juice, freshly
   squeezed

2 teaspoons lemon zest
1 pint whipping cream, whipped
2 dozen ladyfingers, split into
   2 layers
Fresh strawberries and whipped
   cream for garnish

Soften gelatin in water and dissolve over hot water. Separate eggs and beat yolks, adding 1/2 cup sugar gradually. Add salt and beat until thickened. Slowly add lemon juice, zest, and gelatin. Beat egg whites until foamy and gradually add 1/2 cup sugar, beating until stiff peaks form. Fold into yolk mixture. Fold in whipped cream.

Line a springform pan with split ladyfingers. Pour in 1/2 of the custard mixture. Place more ladyfingers on top and cover with rest of custard. Refrigerate overnight. Remove from pan and decorate with strawberries and sweetened whipped cream.

. . . .

strawberry splendor

1 small sponge cake or 6 ladyfingers
3 tablespoons sugar
1-1/4 cups fresh strawberries,
   crushed

3 cups whipping cream
1/4 teaspoon vanilla extract
1 tablespoon chopped pecans

Line springform pan with split ladyfingers or sliced sponge cake. Add sugar to strawberries. Whip cream with vanilla extract. Cover cake with berries. Add a layer of whipped cream. Repeat in layers until all is used. Save part of cream for top of cake. Sprinkle with pecans and chill overnight.

. . . .

lemon icebox cake

12-ounce loaf sponge cake
1/2 cup butter
1 teaspoon grated lemon zest
1/4 cup lemon juice, freshly squeezed

2 cups confectioners sugar
1/4 cup milk, scalded
1/2 pint whipping cream
1 tablespoon pistachio nuts, sliced

Line bottom and sides of an 8-3/4 x 4-1/2 x 2-1/2-inch glass loaf pan with wax paper, extending paper 1/2 inch over sides.

Cut cake into 12 slices. Cream butter with lemon zest until smooth. Stir in lemon juice and sugar alternately. Add hot milk gradually, beating until fluffy. Using 3 cake slices, evenly line bottom of pan. Spread 1/3 of filling evenly over cake. Repeat with cake and filling until all is used, finishing with a layer of cake.

Cover tightly with wax paper. Chill 5 to 6 hours. To serve, lift both pieces of paper overhanging the loaf pan to lift cake to serving plate. Remove paper. Spread top and sides with whipped and sweetened cream. Sprinkle with pistachio nuts.

. . . .

maple pecan cake

1 tablespoon unflavored gelatin
1/2 cup cold water
2 eggs, separated
3/4 cup maple syrup
1/4 teaspoon salt

1 cup whipped cream
10 macaroons, rolled into crumbs
3/4 cup chopped pecans
2 dozen ladyfingers

Soften gelatin in water for 5 minutes. Beat egg yolks slightly. Add maple syrup and salt and cook over boiling water until slightly thickened. Add gelatin and stir until dissolved.

Cool and add whipped cream, macaroon crumbs, and pecans. Fold in stiffly beaten egg whites. Line a mold with separated ladyfingers and fill with maple mixture. Chill.

When firm, unmold and garnish top with sweetened whipped cream. Add pecan halves for garnish, if desired.

. . . .

mocha charlotte

2 envelopes unflavored gelatin
4 tablespoons cold water
3 eggs, separated and beaten
1 cup sugar
1 cup milk

3/4 cup strong brewed coffee
2 tablespoons Kahlua
1 cup whipping cream, whipped
1 dozen ladyfingers, split
Whipped cream (optional)

Soften gelatin in cold water. Combine egg yolks, sugar, milk, and coffee in top of double boiler. Cook, stirring constantly, until mixture coats a spoon. Remove from heat and stir in gelatin. Continue stirring until mixture cools and thickens; fold in stiffly beaten egg whites, whipped cream, and Kahlua. Chill. Line bottom and sides of a springform pan with split ladyfingers. Pour gelatin mixture into pan. Chill until firm. Unmold on chilled cake plate when ready to serve. Serve with sweetened whipped cream, if desired.

. . . .

old fashioned banana wafer cake

1/2 cup sugar
1/4 cup flour
1/4 teaspoon salt
1-1/2 cups milk
2 eggs

2 tablespoons butter
1/2 teaspoon vanilla extract
24 vanilla wafers
3 large ripe bananas
Whipped cream (optional)

Blend sugar, flour, and salt in top of double boiler, stir in milk and cook over hot water until thick, approximately 5 minutes, stirring often. Beat eggs, and add 1/2 cup of the hot mixture and return to double boiler to cook 4 to 5 minutes, stirring constantly. Remove from heat and add butter and vanilla extract. Beat with rotary beater until smooth. Lightly butter an 8-cup round glass casserole. Arrange 9 wafers in bottom of casserole, and spoon 1/2-inch thick layer of custard over wafers. Slice 1 banana over custard and spoon a thin layer of custard over banana.

Lay on 10 wafers, then slice remaining bananas over them. Spread remaining custard over top, completely covering bananas. Crush remaining 5 wafers into fine crumbs and sprinkle over custard. Cover and chill 6 to 8 hours. Serve with sweetened whipped cream, if desired.

orange party cake

1/2 cup sugar
2 teaspoons flour
2 eggs, separated
1/2 cup scalded milk
1 tablespoon butter
Pinch of salt

Grated zest of 1/2 orange
Juice of 1 orange
Ladyfingers or sponge cake cut into
strips
Whipped cream

Mix sugar and flour with beaten egg yolks. Add scalded milk slowly. Add butter and salt and cook in double boiler over hot water until thickened. Add orange zest and juice. Cool slightly and fold in stiffly beaten egg whites.

Place a layer of ladyfingers split lengthwise into a pan lined with wax paper. Spread with orange mixture. Cover with another layer of ladyfingers and continue until mixture is used. Chill overnight. Serve with sweetened whipped cream, if desired.

peach delight

5 eggs, separated
1/2 cup lemon juice
1 cup sugar
1-1/2 envelopes unflavored gelatin

1 cup mashed peaches, canned or
fresh
1 angel food cake
Whipped cream (optional)

Beat the yolks and pour into a double boiler. Add lemon juice and 1/2 cup sugar. Cook until it coats the spoon. Remove from heat and add gelatin which has been dissolved in 1/2 cup water.

Beat egg whites until stiff. Gradually add sugar and beat until soft peaks form. Fold in mashed peaches. Add to custard mixture.

Lightly grease a tube pan with butter. Break the angel food cake in small pieces and arrange a layer of cake topped with custard. Continue to alternate layers and refrigerate at least 4 hours before serving. Remove from pan and slice into serving pieces. Serve with sweetened whipped cream, if desired.

peach dream cake

1 tablespoon unflavored gelatin	1/2 pound marshmallows, cut into
1/4 cup cold water	small pieces
1 cup confectioners sugar	4 cups sliced fresh peaches
1/3 cup butter, softened	2 cups vanilla wafer crumbs
2 eggs, separated	

Soften gelatin in water for 5 minutes. Cream butter and sugar until light and fluffy. Blend in egg yolks well. Cook over low heat, stirring constantly until thickened. Remove from heat, add gelatin and stir until dissolved. Cool slightly. Add marshmallows. Blend lightly and chill until mixture begins to thicken. Fold in peaches and beaten egg whites. Arrange alternate layers of cookie crumbs and peach filling in mold, beginning and ending with cookie crumbs. Chill until firm. Unmold on serving dish. Serve with sweetened whipped cream, if desired.

pineapple crush cake

1-1/4 cups graham cracker crumbs	1 cup sugar
1/4 cup sugar	1/2 cup milk
1/4 cup butter, softened	Pinch of salt
2 envelopes unflavored gelatin	4 cups cottage cheese
1/2 cup cold water	1-1/2 teaspoons grated lemon zest
3 egg yolks	2 tablespoons lemon juice

3 egg whites, stiffly beaten
1 cup canned crushed pineapple, drained
1 cup whipping cream

Combine graham cracker crumbs, 1/4 cup sugar, and butter thoroughly. Reserve 1/3 cup of this mixture. Pack remaining mixture in bottom of a greased 9-inch spring-form pan.

Sprinkle gelatin over cold water. Let stand until softened, approximately 5 minutes.

Beat egg yolks slightly in top of double boiler. Add 1 cup sugar gradually, beating well with rotary beater. Stir in milk and salt. Cook over boiling water, stirring constantly, until slightly thickened and custard coats a spoon. Stir in gelatin until dissolved. Cool slightly.

Press cheese through sieve or beat with electric mixer until smooth. Add lemon zest and juice; mix well. Add slightly cooled custard mixture, beating until thoroughly blended. Let cool until thickened and partially set. Beat with electric or hand mixer until light and foamy. Fold in egg whites, whipped cream, and pineapple.

Pour into crumb-lined pan. Sprinkle top with remaining crumbs. Chill 2 or 3 hours.

peppermint stick charlotte

2 envelopes unflavored gelatin
3/4 cup sugar, divided
1/4 teaspoon salt
4 eggs, separated
2-1/2 cups milk

Red food coloring
2/3 cup finely crushed peppermint
   stick candy
12 ladyfingers
1 cup heavy cream, whipped

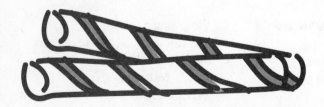

In medium saucepan, mix gelatin, 1/4 cup sugar, and salt.

Beat egg yolks and milk together; stir into gelatin. Place over low heat; stir constantly until gelatin dissolves and mixture thickens slightly, approximately 5 minutes. Remove from heat and cool slightly. Stir in a few drops of red food coloring and crushed candy. Chill, stirring occasionally, until mixture mounds slightly when dropped from a spoon.

While mixture chills, separate ladyfingers and stand them around the inside of a 9-inch springform pan with rounded sides against pan. Beat egg whites until soft peaks form. Gradually beat in remaining 1/2 cup sugar and beat until stiff peaks form. Fold into chilled gelatin mixture. Fold in whipped cream and turn into prepared pan. Chill until set.

To serve, remove from pan and garnish with additional whipped cream and crushed candy.

. . . .

snowball cake

2 envelopes unflavored gelatin
3 tablespoons cold water
1 cup pineapple juice
1 (20-ounce) can crushed pineapple, drained

1 pint whipping cream, sweetened and whipped
1 large angel food cake
1 (7-ounce) can flaked coconut

Mix gelatin with 3 tablespoons cold water. Add 1 cup hot water and pineapple juice. Add pineapple and chill until firm. Fold in whipped cream. Reserve 1/3 of the mixture for topping.

Break cake into large pieces and alternate layers of cake, topping, and coconut in large mold, ending with a layer of cake pieces.

Chill at least 3 hours. Unmold onto a 10-inch cake plate. Spread reserved whipped cream mixture over cake and sprinkle coconut on top.

. . . .

springtime delight

6 eggs, separated
1-1/2 cups sugar, divided
3/4 cup lemon juice
2 teaspoons grated lemon zest

1 envelope gelatin
1/4 cup cold water
1 angel food cake
Whipped cream

Mix egg yolks, 3/4 cup sugar, lemon juice, and zest in top of double boiler and cook until thickened. Dissolve gelatin in water and add to above. Beat egg whites until frothy and gradually add 3/4 cup sugar, beating until stiff peaks form. Fold custard slowly into egg whites.

Line a tube pan with wax paper. Break cake into small pieces and alternate layers of cake and custard in pan. Chill overnight. Approximately 2 hours before serving, spread with whipped cream.

measurements, & equivalents, help ful hints

Have a lot
of fun
today...
bake
a cake!

measurements

Pinch	a few grains, less than 1/8 teaspoon
3 level teaspoons.	1 tablespoon or 1/2 ounce
4 tablespoons	1/4 cup
8 tablespoons	1/2 cup
16 tablespoons	1 cup
1 cup	8 ounces or 1/2 pint
2 cups	16 ounces or 1 pint or 1 pound
2 pints	1 quart
1/2 pound.	1 cup
1/4 pound.	1/2 cup

equivalents

Cocoa:

1 pound	4 cups

Eggs:

2 large	3 small

Evaporated milk:

6-ounce can	3/4 cup
14-1/2-ounce can	1-2/3 cups

Flour:

1 pound all-purpose.	4 cups sifted
1 pound cake.	4-1/2 cups sifted

Nut Meats (coarsely chopped):

1 pound	3-1/2 cups

Sugar:

1 pound granulated	2 cups
1 pound confectioners	3-1/2 cups
1 pound brown	2 cups

Whipping Cream:

1 cup	2 cups whipped

Substitutions:

1 cup sifted cake flour.	1 cup all-purpose flour, minus 2 tablespoons
1 square chocolate.	3 tablespoons cocoa, plus 1 tablespoon vegetable shortening

helpful hints

To measure flour Always sift flour once before measuring. Heap flour lightly into measuring cup with a scoop or spoon, level off top with straight edge of a knife. Never dip a measuring cup into flour, as that packs the flour down. Be careful not to jar or rap filled cup. This causes flour to settle and results in too much flour being used.

To measure sugar Fill measuring cup with granulated or white sugar and level off with straight edge of a knife. Brown sugar should be packed into measuring cup so firmly that it retains its shape when turned out of the cup.

To measure baking powder, soda, salt, spices, etc. Use standard measuring spoon. Fill spoon heaping full, level off with straight edge of a knife.

To measure liquids Place glass measuring cup on a level surface to fill. Pour liquid into cup or measuring container. Do not dip spoon or utensil into container.

Butter or shortening Makes the cake tender. Use a shortening or butter which has a mild sweet flavor and which creams easily.

Sugar Fine granulated sugar is used in all recipes unless otherwise indicated. Coarse sugar makes a coarse-textured cake. Brown sugar and maple sugar add flavor in addition to sweetening a cake.

Eggs Remove eggs from refrigerator several hours before using so that they will beat up to their greatest volume. In separating it is important that none of the yolk gets into the white. Make sure the bowl and beaters are dry and free of oil.

Flour   Two types of flour are used in cake making. Cake flour is made from soft winter wheats and all-purpose flour is made from spring or winter wheats. Cake flour produces a lighter, more tender cake than does all-purpose flour. If all-purpose flour is used instead of cake flour, reduce the amount of flour by 2 tablespoons per cup and avoid over-beating the batter.

Liquid   Milk—sweet or sour—is most commonly used in baking cakes; however, cream, buttermilk, water, fruit juices, and coffee may be also used.

Dried fruits   In recipes calling for dried fruits (dates, raisins, prunes, apricots, etc.) to be cut up, use kitchen scissors dipped occasionally in warm water.

Chocolate hints   Melt chocolate in any of these ways:

1 Place in heavy saucepan over very low heat, stirring until smooth.

2 Place in heat-safe custard cup and set in pan of hot water until melted.

3 Place in top of double boiler and melt over hot water. Do not boil the water as this will curdle the chocolate.

Mix a little unsweetened cocoa in the flour when you are greasing and flouring cake pans for baking chocolate cakes. This will prevent a streaky look.

Handy cocoa substitution: If recipe calls for unsweetened chocolate, use 3 tablespoons cocoa, plus 1 tablespoon shortening or salad oil (NOT butter or margarine) for each 1 ounce of chocolate required.

To test a cake   To test for perfect doneness, pierce the middle of the layer with a wooden skewer or cake tester. If the tester comes out clean when withdrawn, the cake is done.

To make a perfect cake   To make the perfect cake, one you can be proud to serve, use only the freshest and best ingredients, measure accurately, and follow instructions carefully. When you put together a cake, you are creating a miracle. No two cakes are ever exactly alike. How exciting! And what a wonderful adventure in cooking and baking.

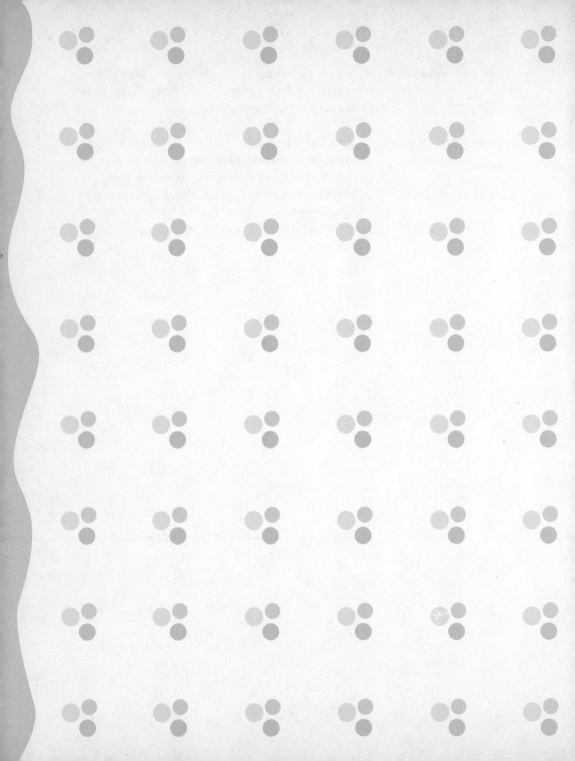

index